JAPANESE
BUREAUCRACY

JAPANESE BUREAUCRACY

Toshimi Sasaki. Prof. Ph. D.

This edition first published by Wiley Publishing Japan K.K. 2019
© 2019 by Toshimi Sasaki

Registered office: Wiley Publishing Japan K.K. – Koishikawa Sakura Bldg. 4F,
1-28-1 Koishikawa Bunkyo-ku, Tokyo 112-0002, Japan.
Tel: +81 3 3830 1221

For details of our editorial offices, for customer services and for information
about how to apply for permission to reuse the copyright material in this book
please see our website at www.wiley.co.jp.

All rights reserved. No part of this publication may be reproduced, stored in a
retrieval system, or transmitted, in any form or by any means, electronic,
mechanical, photocopying, recording or otherwise, without the prior permission
of the publisher.

Designations used by companies to distinguish their products are often claimed
as trademarks. All brand names and product names used in this book are trade
names, service marks, trademarks or registered trademarks of their respective
owners. The publisher is not associated with any product or vendor mentioned
in this book. It is sold on the understanding that the publisher is not engaged
in rendering professional services. If professional advice or other expert
assistance is required, the services of a competent professional should be
sought.

The contents of this work are intended to further general scientific research,
understanding, and discussion only and are not intended and should not be
relied upon as recommending or promoting a specific method, diagnosis, or
treatment by health science practitioners for any particular patient. The
publisher and the author make no representations or warranties with respect to
the accuracy or completeness of the contents of this work and specifically
disclaim all warranties, including without limitation any implied warranties of
fitness for a particular purpose. In view of ongoing research, equipment
modifications, changes in governmental regulations, and the constant flow of
information relating to the use of medicines, equipment, and devices, the reader
is urged to review and evaluate the information provided in the package insert
or instructions for each medicine, equipment, or device for, among other things,
any changes in the instructions or indication of usage and for added warnings
and precautions. Readers should consult with a specialist where appropriate.
The fact that an organization or Website is referred to in this work as a citation
and/or a potential source of further information does not mean that the author
or the publisher endorses the information the organization or Website may
provide or recommendations it may make. Further, readers should be aware
that Internet Websites listed in this work may have changed or disappeared
between when this work was written and when it is read. No warranty may be
created or extended by any promotional statements for this work. Neither the
publisher nor the author shall be liable for any damages arising herefrom.

Printed in Japan

ISBN 978-4-939028-72-4 C3031 Y2700 E

Publication date: 19 April 2019

CONTENTS

About the author	6
Preface	7
Acknowledgments	10
Introduction and Outline	12

Chapter 1　Previous Studies　20
1. Previous Studies in the United States　20
2. Administrative Systems in Japan　26

Chapter 2　Factors Regulating Implementation Processes　32
1. Three Steps in Policymaking　35
2. Public Services and Its Relations with Three Models　41
3. Background of the Hypothesis　47

Chapter 3　Policy Process and Characteristics　54
1. Development of Social Welfare Policy in Japan　54
2. Analysis of Independent Variables　61
3. Policy Process and Hypotheses　66
4. Hypotheses and Characteristics Concerning the Policy　70

Chapter 4　Quality of Policy and Three Models　80
1. Examining the Vertical Determinant Model　80
2. Relation Between Models and Policy Performance　90
3. Consideration of the Results　96

Chapter 5　Decentralization and Policy Process　100
1. Scale of Municipalities and Hypothesis　100
2. Safety Net and Policy Process　107
3. Images of Japanese Bureaucracy　110

References	112

ABOUT THE AUTHOR

The author, Toshimi Sasaki is the Professor of the Heisei International University in Japan. Her research expertise is in comparative public administration and social welfare policy. She is also an active social worker.

PREFACE

Many studies have clarified the mechanisms of Japanese bureaucracy. Some studies have focused on the management system of Japanese public organizations, while others have emphasized the Japanese group-oriented culture called "groupism." However, no studies have focused on the following question: "Why is Japanese bureaucracy strong?"

The Master of Public Administration course at the California State University was insightful. It helped to learn systematized public administration as in the United States and to examine Japanese bureaucracy. Although the basic nature of public administrators is common throughout the world, the culture of public officials is different. Through this experience, I realized that Japanese bureaucracy was strong and that this fundamental system supports the daily lives of people.

This is not a new discovery but a kind of common knowledge for many researchers of public administration. However, no studies have focused on the following question: "How can Japanese bureaucracy strongly influence Japanese society?." The historical aspect, which emphasizes that the Japanese society has been controlled by public administrators for a long time, and the cultural aspect, which considers Japan as a high trust society vis-a-vis public administrators, are important for answering this question. However, in my opinion, the systematic aspect of public decision making makes Japanese bureaucracy influential in society. Basic systems, which support not only the daily lives of people but also businesses and/or the economy, have been established by bureaucrats. The implementation of public policies is completely controlled by public officials[1]. Centralized and decentralized systems does not significantly influence Japanese bureaucracy because both systems are established by public administrators[2]. Bureaucrats greatly influence the society via either system, thereby creating a strong Japanese bureaucracy.

In the global era, people have begun to realize that several rules and systems that work well for a long time are no longer perfect and that a peculiar value or standard may not solve worldwide problems. Top leaders in political and public spheres as well as ordinary people should utilize "multiple perspectives[3]" to communicate with foreigners worldwide and solve problems. The multiple perspective approach is considered to be important in the United States and Japan. This proves that people worldwide face similar problems, thereby prompting the following assertion: "Existing systems no longer work well, so we should make new one!" Decentralization processes in public areas in Japan can be evaluated as one of the

---

[1] Bureaucracy means all public administrators in public administration. In Japan, it refers to public administrators in the central government. Public administrators in local governments do not have much power to establish the policy; rather, they implement the policy of the center. Thus, public administrators in local governments have been called "public officials" and not "bureaucrats." I distinguish bureaucracy and public officials in this book since the word "public administrators" is used to mean both.

[2] Presently in Japan, decentralization reform is going on rapidly. The purpose is to empower public officials in local governments to establish their own policies. The strength of the relation between the center and local areas will be gradually changed through this reform. However, in either centralized or decentralized societies, public administrators still greatly influence businesses and the daily lives of people.

[3] The multiple perspective approach is an important concept in the Master of Public Administration course. Public administrators should have broader perspectives to solve global problems, and having multiple perspectives is the best method for this purpose.

Preface

main systematic changes brought by the multiple perspective approach, and this book is written from this perspective.

This book clarifies the mechanisms of Japanese bureaucracy through multiple perspectives. It focuses on the establishment and implementation of public policies. Using several aggregate datasets and the results of much published research, I focus on one simple question: "Why is Japanese bureaucracy strong?" I hope this book contributes to the study of public administration.

ACKNOWLEDGMENTS

In 1997, I met Dr. Jong S. Jun, the former department chair at California State University, Hayward (CSUH), for the first time while studying the Master of Public Administration (MPA) course. I chose to study the MPA course because though public administration has been studied by many researchers in Japan, it has not been systematized as in the United States. Public administrators in Japan acquire practical knowledge of public administration through job trainings after obtaining jobs within public organizations. The science of public administration focuses on the bureaucratic system. However, through the MPA program at CSUH, I could learn a totally systematized form of public administration, including mechanisms of bureaucracy, skills for organization management, and several public policies, all of which fascinated me. From this experience, I decided to major in public administration after returning to Japan.

The professors at CSUH assisted me during my study as well as guided me in the United States for two years. Dr. Jong S. Jun was my academic adviser, and he and his wife supported me in my daily life in California. They were instrumental in helping me complete the MPA program and publish this book. Furthermore, Dr. Yanow assisted me through various classes. Her theory of interpreted public policy considerably influenced me. After I returned to Japan, she guided me during my research paper on educational policy in Japan. I would like to extend my sincere gratitude to Dr Morgan, Dr Umeh, Dr. Dennard, and Mrs. Anne Marter for their generous support from the beginning of my study.

Acknowledgments

I began to write this book on the basis of the study of public administration in California. I have added several analyses and practical research issues relating to Japanese bureaucracy. I appreciate the support of Dr. Kobayashi, a professor at Keio University, who was my academic advisor after returning to Japan. He assisted me during my doctoral program for five years. I obtained my PHD and wrote this book under his guidance.

I hope this book aids foreign researchers to understand Japanese bureaucracy and contributes to the study of public administration.

INTRODUCTION
AND OUTLINE

It is important to focus on the differences in systems among countries as well as the associated political culture that greatly influences the bureaucratic system. We should first understand the political culture of Japan to understand the mechanisms by which Japanese bureaucracy strongly influences society. Society is in a state of continual transformation, and Japanese society is no exception. Accordingly, comparing a country's political culture with other different cultures will be the most useful way to understand the political culture of a country in terms of its history and current configuration. Thus, I focus on a comparative study of political culture between the United States and Japan before the main discussion.

Numerous studies have noted that Japanese society is shifting from being a centralized country to a more decentralized one such as the United States. Both centralized and decentralized systems have their own merits and drawbacks. Therefore, we cannot easily evaluate which system is superior to the other. In its era of being a centralized society, Japan tried to obtain a "national minimum standard" of public services. The main focus points of public administrators included the following: (1) to standardize the quality and quantity of public services; (2) to fairly distribute public services to all the people in Japan; and (3) to use strong leadership of the central government to lead the local ones. In most policy

Introduction and Outline 13

areas, the Japanese central government used strong central power to rule over local governments to obtain the minimum standard of public services in all districts in Japan. Social welfare policy has been no exception. The central government treated social welfare policy as a "national matter" and not as a "local problem." It tried to establish a society where all Japanese citizens were able to obtain the same levels of welfare regardless of job status and living area. The centralized administration system of Japanese society was suitable for realizing such a society with a standardized level of social welfare policy.

However, for a long time, many bureaucrats in Japan were increasingly aware of the demerits of this system. Although we have the Local Autonomy Law and approximately 3000 local governments, these do not work well in a centralized society such as Japan. Consequently, the following conditions have transpired: (1) public services are always given on the same basis under different conditions; (2) Japanese people do not have the consciousness of local autonomy; and (3) people do not have the power to control the governments. During the period of transformation from a developing nation mainly constituting villages to a more modernized society, the centralized public system can be gauged as the most suitable one. However, in modern countries with democratic political systems, people should have the consciousness and the powers of local autonomy. Public services should be provided by public administrators, and citizens should have the power to choose the quality and quantity of public services. With the enforcement of the new Local Autonomy Law in Japan in April 2000, Japanese society has been gradually changing into a more decentralized one.

A decentralized public system has three merits that do not pertain to centralized mechanisms. These are as follows: (1) quickness of decision making in public policy; (2) totality of public services in several policy areas; and (3) variation in terms of public policies. Japanese bureaucrats have evaluated these merits of a decentralized society and have established the law to empower local governments so that people control the public policy through participation in policy processes. In other words, citizens have begun to consider the variation and totality of public services to be more important than the standardized public policies. By establishing the decentralized public system and empowering local governments, the central government focused on foreign policies. Public policies in municipalities began to be established and implemented by public officials in local governments. Simultaneously, people received more variation in terms of services and had greater choice and power to control them. The National Committee for Decentralization, which was established with the enforcement of the new Local Autonomy Law, mentioned five merits of decentralization. These included the following: (1) the central government should not have the power to control domestic public matters; (2) local governments should offer more variety in public services with their own will; (3) local areas should become more wealthy; (4) political systems should be more efficient and less corrupt; and (5) people and companies in Tokyo should be more dispersed toward several suburban areas[1]. By reforming the centralized system to a more decentralized one, the following will occur: (1) some local

---

[1] The National Committee of Decentralization established the Interim Report in March 1993 and mentioned these five points in it.

governments will not be able to obtain the national minimum standards of public services; (2) the unity and totality of public services cannot be maintained; and (3) the central government will no longer be able to use strong power to govern local ones. Currently, many public administrators evaluate the merits of a decentralized system more than its demerits.

Centralized Society

1. Centralized non-Cooperative	2. Centralized Cooperative
(e.g. Japan before World War II)	(e.g. France, Germany, and Japan after World War II)
3. Decentralized non-Cooperative	4. Decentralized Cooperative
(e.g. U.S.A and U.K.)	(e.g. North European Countries)

Decentralized Society

(This figure was drawn using the discussion of Nishio in 1993[2])

There are different types of public systems in the world, and both centralized and decentralized societies can be classified into four types of systems. As Nishio mentioned[2], societies can be classified into four typologies by using two types of standards (see **Figure 1-1** in Chapter 1).

The first standard is the "jurisdiction of power." This means determining which government, central or local, has strong power to control decision making in public policy formation and implementation. In centralized countries, the jurisdiction of power belongs to the central government; in decentralized countries, local governments have more decision-making

---

[2] Nishio, M., *Public Administration*, Yuhikaku Press, 1993, pp. 57-65.

powers. The next standard is "cooperation between the central and local governments." In some countries, many public policies are established by both central and local governments via mutual cooperation. In other countries, only central or local governments can make their own decisions within their respective jurisdictions. Using these two standards, societies can thus be classified into four typologies.

1. Centralized non-cooperative systems exist in societies where the central government can totally control the decision-making process of public policy. Local governments have no local autonomy. Japan had this type of public system before World War II.

2. Decentralized non-cooperative systems exist in societies where local governments can establish many public policies and have power to implement them in their jurisdictions. In these countries, cooperation between central and local governments is relatively low, and both make their own decisions. The United States and the United Kingdom have this system.

3. Centralized cooperative systems exist in societies where the central government has strong power to establish public policies. Local governments implement these policies in their jurisdictions by following the guidelines and standards of the central government. There is little autonomy in these types of local governments. France, Germany, and Japan after the World War II have this type of system.

4. Decentralized cooperative systems exist in societies where both central and local governments can establish their own decisions, but the cooperation between these governments

is high. Some north European countries belong to this typology, but only a few countries in the world have this kind of system.

Presently in Japan, public administrators are considering ways in which Japanese bureaucracy should function. Accordingly, which of the decentralized systems, decentralized non-cooperative system or centralized cooperative system, is more suitable for Japanese political culture[3]?

Japanese bureaucracy, the main focus of this book, is now dramatically changing and has had several different characteristics in various periods and in many policy areas. However, the basic system of Japanese bureaucracy still exists and cannot be changed so easily even by the bureaucrats. Therefore, in this book, I analyze the characteristics and mechanisms of Japanese bureaucracy by focusing on the social welfare policy area.

OVERVIEW OF THE BOOK

Chapter 1 reviews preceding studies on innovative processes of public policymaking in states and local governments within the United States. Because local autonomy is high and local governments can establish and implement their own public policies freely in the United States, there have been numerous studies on the diffusion process of new public policies. Because the strong influence of Japanese bureaucracy on society is fundamentally related to the mechanisms of diffusion processes,

---

[3] After World War 2, the GHQ mentioned that the Japanese government should have the decentralized non-cooperative type of system.

it is valuable to use some models in these prior studies for analyzing Japanese bureaucracy.

Chapter 2 clarifies the three main models used to analyze Japanese bureaucracy in this book. The "internal determinant model" symbolizes the policy process in which needs of residents and policies of municipalities are greatly influenced by the introduction of new public policies. The "regional diffusion model" symbolizes the policy process in which innovation processes are influenced by the interaction of municipalities. The "vertical determinant model" symbolizes the policy process in which the relationship of the upper level of governments is influenced by the policy process of the local governments. In this book, discussions and analyses are generated in relation to these three models, and I explain these models in detail in Chapter 2 by using the research and interviews of three municipalities.

In Chapter 3, social welfare policy is the main topic of discussion. I clarify both independent variables and dependent variables for statistical analysis in this policy area. The main focus of the analysis is to clarify the variables that directly influence the quantity of public services in each municipality. The results of the statistical analyses of this chapter clarify the relation among applicable models, concrete policy processes, and characteristics of programs in social welfare policy. The more fundamental characteristics the policies and programs have, the more suitable the vertical determinant model becomes. In contrast, the more progressive characteristics the policies and programs have, the more applicable the internal determinant model becomes. In Japan, the regional determinant model fits all the programs in the social welfare policy area.

Introduction and Outline 19

In Chapter 4, the quality, not quantity, of the social welfare policy is the main focus of consideration. Through statistical analysis, I clarify the relation between the quality of services and the three models. In other words, using the results of the consciousness research as well as interview researches in three preceding municipalities, I clarify which model or policy process is most desirable for residents in municipalities to obtain the most preferable public services for their region.

In Chapter 5, I consider the future direction of Japanese bureaucracy, with its changes under the decentralization reforms, and clarify the prospective mechanisms of Japanese bureaucracy. As shown by the results of analysis in former chapters, the internal determinant policy process is most preferable for the residents in municipalities, but the vertical determinant policy process has been dominant in most Japanese municipalities. Therefore, the final chapter clarifies the policies that transform Japanese bureaucracy into a more desirable one by mentioning the possibility of regional determinant policy process and examines the general concept of Japanese bureaucracy.

CHAPTER 1

PREVIOUS STUDIES

1. PREVIOUS STUDIES IN THE UNITED STATES

Preceding studies on the innovation process of public policies in local governments are rich in the United States. In the United States, local autonomy is high and local governments can establish and implement their own public policies freely compared with those in other centralized countries. Jack L. Walker[1] first focused on the diffusion of innovations among the American States in 1969. He clarified why new public policies were introduced and propagated speedily in some states and slowly in others. He analyzed the introduction mechanism of 88 programs in local governments in policy areas such as accounts, traffic, environment, and social welfare and established the "innovation score." The main focus of this research was to clarify why new public policies were speedily introduced in states such as New York, California, and Michigan and slowly introduced in Mississippi State and South Dakota State. Furthermore, he established correlations among the innovation score, demographic factors, and political factors to determine the mechanisms of innovation. He found that states with high income levels and innovative factories introduced

---

[1] Jack L. Walker, "The Diffusion of Innovations among the American States", *American Political Science Review*, vol.63, 1969, pp.880-899.

new policies. In addition, he used the factor analysis method to compare the innovation scores of several states and found that the innovativeness of some states varied dramatically and greatly influenced other states.

After Walker uncovered the mechanisms of diffusion processes of innovations among states, similar studies were successfully undertaken. Virginia Gray[2] examined Walker's definition more carefully and analyzed the innovation of new public laws on education, social welfare, and civil rights. She established the model in which new public laws were pervaded through the interaction of states and proved this fact by using 12 cases of the introduction of new public laws. Grupp and Richards[3] expanded Walker's research to relate the findings to state expenditure studies. Their focus was whether bureaucrats were influenced by the trends of other states. They analyzed the policymaking process in bureaucracies. They divided large bureaucracies into 10 bureaus, i.e., education, public works, natural resources, business regulation, human relations, welfare, auxiliary, and conducted consciousness researches for these 10 different types of bureaucrats. These researches focused on factors within local governments to clarify the mechanisms of innovation, and this idea began to be called "internal determinant model." Savage[4] focused on policy innovativeness and established the measure of the speed of adoption for a state policy by using 181 different types of

---

[2] Virginia Gray, "Innovation in the States: A Diffusion Study", *American Political Science Review*, vol.67, 1973, pp.1174-1193.
[3] Fred W. Grupp Jr. and Alan R. Richards, "Variations in Elite Perceptions of American States As Referents for Public Policy Making", *American Political Science Review*, vol.69, 1975, pp.850-858.
[4] Robert L. Savage, "Policy Innovation as a Trait of American States," *Journal of Politics*, vol.40, 1978, pp.212-224.

public laws. In these four types of researches on diffusion processes, interaction among neighboring municipalities greatly influenced the diffusion process of innovations, and this idea came to be called the "regional diffusion model."

In late 1970s, research on diffusion and innovation proceeded through two different approaches. One approach was to clarify the variables of models, and the other was to establish the new model to compare different models with regard to the same phenomenon.

Collier and Messick[5] established the comparative study of diffusion between the internal determinant model and regional diffusion model. The main focus of their research was to clarify which model was more effective, the "internal determinant model" or the "regional diffusion model." The analysis focused on two of the most important explanations of social security development: 1. the prerequisites explanation, which emphasizes causes of social security development within nations, most commonly at the level of social and economic modernization and 2. diffusion, which focused on the imitation of social security programs among nations. In conclusion, they noted that hierarchical diffusion was present, with later adopters tending to adopt at far lower levels of modernization than the early adopters.

Robert Eyestone[6] insisted that the innovation process cannot be explained only by one model but by several models of policy diffusion operating simultaneously. He mentioned more than

---

[5] David Collier and Richard E. Messick, "Prerequisites Versus Diffusion: Testing Alternative Explanations of Social Security Adoption", *American Political Science Review*, vol. 69, 1975, pp.1299-1315.
[6] Robert Eyestone, "Confusion, Diffusion, and Innovation", *American Political Science Review*, vol.71, 1977, pp.441-447.

one possible pattern of emulation of policy innovations. Furthermore, he presented a technique for identifying clusters of similar policies on the basis of the diffusion patterns observed by using fair employment practices, civil rights, and labor legislation. He examined the history of state minimum wage legislation and showed the importance of repeals, amendments, and reinstatements in addition to initial adoptions. Berry and Berry[7] insisted that the two types of explanations of state government innovation were conceptually compatible, relying on Mohr's theory of organizational innovation. These include the internal determinant model, which posits that the factors causing a state government to innovate are political, economic, and social characteristics of a state, and regional diffusion models, which point toward the role of policy adoptions by neighboring states. They developed and tested a unified explanation of state lottery adoptions. They reflected on both internal and regional influences and concluded that the empirical results provided a great degree of support for Mohr's theory. They used event history analysis, a form of pooled cross-sectional time series analysis. E. M. Rogers[8] systematized several types of innovation researches in political science, sociology, and medical science.

Concerning the regional diffusion model, Harold Wolman[9] examined the response of local governments to fiscal austerity. He examined the innovation research literature with respect to

[7] Berry, Francis Stokes, and William D. Berry, "State Lottery Adoptions as Policy Innovations: An Event History Analysis", *American Political Science Review*, vol.84, 1990, pp.822-840.
[8] Rogers, Everett M., *Diffusion of Innovations*, New York: The Free Press, 3rd Edidion, 1983.
[9] Harold Wolman, "Innovation in Local Government and Fiscal Austerity", *Journal of Public Policy*, vol.6, no.,1986, pp.159-180.

each of these questions to determine the findings or hypotheses that emerge from this existing body of research and those that are relevant to these newly formulated questions. He used several detailed variables such as environment (which includes political factors); socioeconomic factors; community attitudes (and other community characteristics); interorganizational relations and structural characteristics (which includes decentralization, flexibility, lack of formalization); and complexity vis-à-vis the characteristics of individuals in organizations. Feiock and Clingermayer[10] used four variables, i.e., executive veto, government form, election, and representation, to examine the relation with economic development activities in local governments. They found that executive power is positively related to tax abatements and UDAG activities.

Eliza K. Pavalko[11] focused on workmen's compensation while studying state timing of policy adoption. According to the results of her analysis, states were quicker to adopt legislation when productivity and work-accident litigation were high and when non-agricultural workers outnumbered agricultural ones. Despite the influence of capital and labor in shaping workmen's compensation in other analyses, the speed of state legislation was unaffected by the presence or interests of capital and labor groups. This suggests that the speed of adoption was shaped by different aspects of capital–labor relations than is seen when studies focus on the activities of specific actors or groups.

---

[10] Feiock, Richard C. and James Clingermayer, "Municipal Representation, Executive Power and Economic Development Policy Activity, *Policy Studies Journal*, vol.15, 1986, pp.211-231.

[11] Eliza K. Pavalko, "State Timing of Policy Adoption: Workmen's Compensation in the United States, 1909-1929", *American Journal of Sociology*, vol.95, no.3, November 1989, pp.592-615.

Bowman and Kearney[12] focused on the important policy areas of economic development, education, and toxic and radioactive waste. They constructed a model identifying the elements of the resurgence, its products, and its potential depressors within the respective states. They discussed different policy areas from an innovation perspective. Economic development, education, hazardous waste, and unclear waste were explored to discover what the 50 experimental laboratories known as the states were doing.

In the 1990s, many studies on policy diffusion focused at the local level; however, most did so at the state level. Feiock and West[13] mentioned that while much focus had been placed on policy adoption at the state level, there was a lack of similar research on policy adoption at the local government level. They explored a set of variables based on alternative conceptions of municipal policymaking to explore differences between different cities' adoption of residential curbside recycling programs and their failure to adopt policy changes. Probit analysis found empirical support for explanations of policy adoption based on need, party competition, fiscal capacity, and interest group organizations. They established and compared seven models: need/responsive policymaking model, diffusion-of-innovation model, political institutions model, federalism model, economic model, interest group influence model, and administrative capacity model.

---

[12] Bowman, Ann O'M., and Richard Kearney, *The Resurgence of the States*, Englewood Cliffs, NJ:Prentice Hall, 1986.
[13] Richard C. Feiock, and Johathan P. West, Testing Competing Explanations for Policy Adoption: Municipal Solid Waste Recycling Programs, *Political Research Quarterly*, 1992, pp. 399-419.

26   Chapter 1

In Japan, only a few studies have explored diffusion. In the social welfare policy area, Tukahara[14] compared the regional diffusion model and internal determinant model in Tokyo. He concluded that regional diffusion model is more applicable to the diffusion process of social welfare services in Tokyo area. Ito[15] focused on the policy diffusion process of four different policy areas. He found that the applicable model can change depending on whether the central government intervenes in the decision-making process of local governments.

2. ADMINISTRATIVE SYSTEMS IN JAPAN

A local public entity, which includes both municipalities and prefectures, is a corporation created on the basis of specified areas within the national territory. Its membership is given to residents therein; its basic function is to control public administration within its area to be of benefit to the residents based on the right of autonomy as recognized by the central government. A local public entity is given the status of a public corporation by the Local Autonomy Law[16].

The Local Autonomy Law divides local public entities into two major categories: ordinary local public entities and special local public entities. Subdivisions of these categories are described in **Figure 1-1**.

---

[14] TsukaharaY., "*Diffusion of Social Welfare Policy*", Study of Social Welfare, vol.28, no. 2, 1992, pp.26-48. (Japanese)
[15] Ito S., *Diffusion Process*, Keio University Press, 2002. (Japanese)
[16] Whole description of this session is based on the following book; Naruse, N. and Isozaki, Y, *The Local Administration in Japan*, Gyosei, 1997.

Local Public Entities	Ordinary Local Public Entities	Prefectures 47	To	1 (Tokyo-to)
			Do	1 (Hokkai-do)
			Fu	2 (Osaka-fu, Kyoto-fu)
			Ken	43
		Municipalities 3,232	Shi (Cities)	669
			Cho (Towns)	1,993
			Son (Villages)	570
	Special Local Public Entities		Special Wards	23
			Cooperatives of Local Public Entities	2,820
			Local Development Corporations	10
			Property Wards	4,244

Figure 1-1 Subdivisions of Local Public Entities

A. Ordinary Local Public Entities

Ordinary local public entities are general local public entities relevant to the country. They are established to advance the welfare of their residents. The current local government system adopts a two-tiered system of prefectures and municipalities.

Prefectures are wide-based local public entities comprising municipalities. Municipalities are basic local public entities situated within the residents' locale. They take charge of all local administration, except for matters handled by prefectures. The following affairs are under the control of prefectures:

(1) Affairs that cover a wide area, such as the preparation of overall development plans for regional, mountain, and river development.

(2) Affairs that require overall uniformity, such as maintenance of the established standard of compulsory (and other) education, and the administration and operation of a police force.

(3) Affairs that relate to the liaison and coordination of municipalities, such as relations between the national government and municipalities.

(4) Affairs that exceed the level at which municipalities are deemed to be capable of handling properly, such as the establishment and maintenance of senior high schools, laboratories, and museums.

Compared with the organizations and functions of Cho (Town) and Son (Village), no major differences were observed in those of Shi (City). Although having a larger number of assembly members, the compulsory appointment of a treasurer and compulsory establishment of social welfare offices are features unique to a city. A large population and more urbanized characteristics distinguish a city from a town and a village.

Table 1-1 Population and Area of Prefectures

(Unit: 1,000 persons, km²)

Name	Population	Area	Name	Population	Area
Hokkaido	5,692	83,452	Shiga	1,287	4,017
Aomori	1,482	9,606	Kyoto	2,630	4,612
Iwate	1,419	15,278	Osaka	8,797	1,892
Miyagi	2,329	7,285	Hyogo	5,402	8,387
Akita	1,214	11,612	Nara	1,431	3,691
Yamagata	1,257	9,323	Wakayama	1,080	4,724
Fukushima	2,134	13,783	Tottori	615	3,507
Ibaraki	2,956	6,094	Shimane	771	6,707
Tochigi	1,984	6,408	Okayama	1,951	7,111
Gunma	2,004	6,363	Hiroshima	2,882	8,475
Saitama	6,759	3,797	Yamaguchi	1,556	6,110
Chiba	5,798	5,156	Tokushima	832	4,144
Tokyo	11,774	2,187	Kagawa	1,027	1,875
Kanagawa	8,246	2,414	Ehime	1,507	5,675
Niigata	2,488	12,582	Kochi	817	7,104
Toyama	1,123	4,246	Fukuoka	4,933	4,968
Ishikawa	1,180	4,185	Saga	884	2,439
Fukui	827	4,188	Nagasaki	1,545	4,091
Yamanashi	882	4,465	Kumamoto	1,860	7,402
Nagano	2,194	13,585	Oita	1,231	6,337
Gifu	2,100	10,598	Miyazaki	1,176	7,734
Shizuoka	3,738	7,779	Kagoshima	1,798	9,186
Aichi	6,868	5,150	Okinawa	1,237	2,266
Mie	1,841	5,774			
			Total	**125,570**	**377,764**

Notes: Population data is based on the 1995 national census (as of Oct. 1, 1995).

Areas are based on the data compiled by the Geographical Survey Institute of the Ministry of Construction (as of Oct.1, 1995).

Source: Naruse, N. and Isozaki, Y., *The Local Administration in Japan*, Gyosei, 1997, p.12.

Table 1-2 Municipalities Classified by Population Size

Population	Year								
	1955	1960	1965	1970	1975	1980	1985	1990	1995
Cities									
1,000,000 or over	5	6	7	8	9	10	10	10	10
500,000 ~ 999,999	2	3	5	6	8	7	9	9	9
300,000 ~ 499,999	7	12	15	23	34	46	38	42	45
200,000 ~ 299,999	21	21	27	39	40	44	39	39	36
100,000 ~ 199,999	63	71	77	78	84	93	105	106	117
50,000 ~ 99,999	140	156	167	178	208	210	221	224	221
under 50,000	253	287	263	265	262	247	229	225	225
Towns & Villages									
30,000 or over	54	34	44	38	37	60	81	100	112
20,000 ~ 29,999	269	280	249	225	223	228	239	233	221
10,000 ~ 19,999	1,126	1,194	1,006	1,953	1,851	1,799	1,735	1,663	1,599
5,000 ~ 9,999	1,435	1,118	1,144	436	502	522	547	594	640
under 5,000	1,438	329	372						
Total	**4,813**	**3,511**	**3,376**	**3,249**	**3,257**	**3,256**	**3,253**	**3,245**	**3,235**

Note: The 23 special wards of Tokyo are counted as one city.

Source: Naruse, N. and Isozaki, Y., *The Local Administration in Japan*, Gyosei, 1997, p.20.

B. Special Local Public Entities

Special wards, cooperatives of local governments, property wards, and local development corporations are called special local public entities. These special local public entities were created so that its area, organization, and functions are limited when compared with those of ordinary local public entities and are not nationwide.

CHAPTER 2
FACTORS REGULATING IMPLEMENTATION PROCESSES

Some models of policy diffusion help to analyze the mechanisms of Japanese bureaucracy. This is because the strong influence of Japanese bureaucracy on society is completely related to the unique system of policy diffusion process between the central and local governments. Therefore, this chapter clarifies the models used in this book in relation to the preceding models in various other studies on diffusion.

First, I focus on the factors regulating the implementation processes of public policies in local governments. Second, I classify these factors into three different models. These models are fundamentally related to the hypotheses of analysis in this book. I closely examine these in the later part of this chapter.

According to Ito[1], the regulatory factors of policy process are generally classified into inner and outer factors. The inner factors are related to the characteristics of municipalities. These include the relevant economic, social, and political factors of the municipalities. The outer factors influence the relationship between the central and local governments. These include financial aid from the central government, several kinds of regulations, relationships among other municipalities,

---

[1] Ito S., *op.cit.* p.63.

Factors Regulating Implementation Processes

and information from the press. Social welfare policy, the main policy area focused on in this book, is not an exception, and its decision-making process is also considerably influenced by these factors (see **Figure 2-1**).

As previously noted, in the United States, the innovation processes of new public policies are greatly influenced by the "internal determinant model" and the "regional diffusion model." However, in Japan, the relationship between the central and local governments considerably impacts the policy process. We cannot discuss the mechanisms of Japanese bureaucracy without the idea of vertical relationships among governments. Therefore, I use the third model, called the "vertical determinant model." This model indicates the vertical relationship among governments. It depicts the upper level of governments. This implies the central government for prefectures and both the central government and prefectures for municipalities. In this book, discussions and analysis are garnered via these three models.

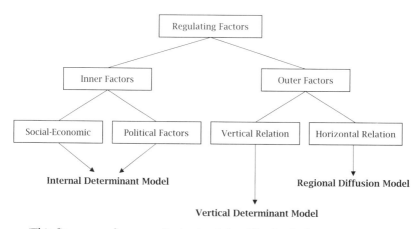

(This figure was drawn on the basis of classification by Ito, *op.cit.* p.63)

Figure 2-1 Factors Regulating Decision-Making Process

(1) Internal determinant model

Factors causing local governments to innovate are political, economic, and social characteristics of municipalities.

(2) Regional diffusion model

Neighboring municipalities play an important role for local governments to adopt new policies.

(3) Vertical determinant model

The strength of relationship between the central and local governments greatly influences the policy adoption of local governments.

The vertical determinant model can be classified into two types: the voluntary vertical determinant model and compulsory vertical determinant model. The "voluntary" model means that public officials in local governments follow the policy of the central government as per their own will because municipalities can either get merits or avoid demerits from the center by its return. Therefore, in this case, municipalities are systematically able to establish their own rules and policies freely, but they are not willing to do it; rather, they follow the intention of the center as per their own will. The "compulsory" model differs from the former in that public officials in local governments have to follow the intention of the central government against their will because of the system of decision making. Even if municipalities would like to establish their own laws or policies, it is difficult to do so because of the budgetary system, human system, strict laws, and various regulations. Therefore, in the later part of this book, I classify the vertical determinant model into two types and clarify which type is more appropriate for analyzing Japanese bureaucracy.

(3)-1: Voluntary Vertical Determinant Model

Public officials in local governments follow the policy of the central government by themselves to get some merits from the center or to avoid demerits from it by its return.

(3)-2: Compulsory Vertical Determinant Model

Public officials in local governments have to follow the intention of the central government against their will because of the system of decision making, such as, strict laws, financial aid, and regulations.

1. THREE STEPS IN POLICYMAKING

First, I consider the relation among the three models, which are described above, and three steps in the policymaking process.

A. First Step: Introduction of a New Policy

The first step in policymaking process is adopting a new public policy or establishing new laws. Whether local governments introduce new policies and when they adopt them are fundamental matters. Three models, which will be used in various situations, will fit well into this first step because these models were fundamentally created to analyze policy adoption. Since local governments have different characteristics, I consider these three models according to the scale and ability of decision making of municipalities.

(1) Internal determinant model

Only few municipalities are applicable to this model.

The ability of policymaking of municipalities applicable to this model is high

The scale of municipalities applicable to this model is large

Introducing new policies, such as opening information to the public or improving the quality of public services, are the typical cases to which the internal determinant model are most applicable. This model is applicable only for a few advanced municipalities in Japan.

(2) Regional determinant model

A moderate number of municipalities are applicable to this model

The ability of policymaking of municipalities applicable to this model is moderate.

The scale of municipalities applicable to this model is moderate

In this case, municipalities with moderate scale, moderate fundamental abilities of policymaking, and those located comparatively close to the preceding municipalities adopt new policies smoothly by imitation.

(3) Vertical determinant model

Numerous municipalities are applicable to this model

The ability of policymaking of municipalities applicable to this model is low.

The scale of municipalities applicable to this model is small

This model is applicable for most small municipalities and villages in Japan. Here, public officials follow the policy of the central government and guarantee the minimum level of public services to residents within their jurisdictions.

B. Second Step: Decision of the Quantity of Public Services (A new policy is already introduced)

The second step is to decide the quantity of the public services to be implemented. After the new policy is introduced in municipalities in the first step, public officials in local governments have to decide the quality of public services in relation to the budget and policy needs of residents. In this book, I apply three models to this second step. These models were originally created to study innovation processes of public policies. As I previously mentioned, social welfare policy is complicated. This is because whether municipalities have the power to implement policy, the quantity and quality of the services markedly influences the daily lives of residents. Accordingly, I use these models to intensively analyze the mechanisms of the second step in policymaking.

B-1 The case in which policy needs of residents are fundamentally fulfilled

(1) Internal determinant model

The quantity of public services to be implemented in municipalities is decided by the size of the budget or strong leadership of the mayor.

(2) Regional determinant model

The quality of public services is suppressed at the lower level because public officials keep services at the level similar to those implemented in neighboring municipalities.

(3) Vertical determinant model

The quantity of public services is compulsorily decided by the central government, and local governments have to follow it. In case municipalities do not have the ability to implement the national minimum level of public services, the central government gives grants to the local government. In cases where the central government is not willing to implement a high level of public services, it does not give grants to local government, and the quantity of public services is compulsorily suppressed at the low level in villages and small towns.

This is the case in which policy needs of residents are fundamentally fulfilled. This is concretely the case with nursing homes. In most municipalities in Japan, the need for nursing homes for elderly residents is high and existing nursing homes are already mostly filled to capacity. In this case, most municipalities want to establish as many nursing homes as possible. Thus, budgetary size and capacity and/or strong leadership of a regional mayor vis-à-vis social welfare policy is the main determinant for deciding the quantity of public services. In other words, although almost all municipalities would like to establish as many new nursing homes as possible, it will obviously cost a lot. Only municipalities with large budgets or whose mayors are willing to put high priority on social welfare policy are able to establish new nursing homes. Other municipalities cannot build new nursing homes although many residents need them. In cases where some municipalities have several nursing homes, neighboring municipalities are not willing to establish new nursing homes within their own jurisdictions because they can use the nursing homes in neighboring municipalities. Therefore, in this case, the regional determinant model can be considered to be undesirable because the quantity of public services is suppressed at the lower level. The vertical determinant model can be either a good or bad one depending on the amount of grants received from the central government.

B-2 The case in which residents' policy needs are completely different among municipalities

(1) Internal determinant model

The quantity of public services to be implemented in municipalities is determined by the policy needs of residents within their jurisdictions.

(2) Regional determinant model

The quality of public services is pushed up to a higher level because public officials keep services at the level similar to those implemented in neighboring municipalities.

(3) Vertical determinant model

The quality of public services is compulsory decided by the central government, and local governments have to follow it. In cases where municipalities do not have the ability to implement a high level of public services, the central government gives grants to the local government. In cases where the central government is not willing to implement high levels of public services, it does not give grants to local governments, and the quantity of public services is compulsory suppressed at the low level in villages and small towns.

This is the case in which policy needs of residents are quite different among municipalities. This is concretely the case of welfare services that provide care for the elderly at home. In most municipalities in Japan, needs for nursing homes for residents are high, while home help services are not so popular. In many municipalities, although local governments improve several services for caring for the elderly at home, residents are not willing to use them. Therefore, in this case, the main determinants that considerably impact the quality of services are the willingness of people to use home help service, the percentage of elderly living with their children, the percentage of people having their own home, the percentage of working women, and cultural factors among residents. In this case, the regional diffusion model will be suitable because neighboring municipalities have to cooperate to improve welfare services for caring for the elderly at home. The vertical determinant model can be either a good or bad one depending on the amount of national grants from the central government.

C. Third Step: Improvement of the Quality of Public Services
(Quantity of public services has already been fulfilled)

Both step one and step two are related to the quantity of public services. This third step relates to the quality of services. This step concerns the period after policy needs of residents have already been fulfilled. Although it is possible to apply these three models to the third step, I focus only on the quantity of public services in this book because the quantity and the quality of social services are quite different. Including analysis for quality will make the discussion complicated.

2. PUBLIC SERVICES AND ITS RELATIONS WITH THREE MODELS

In preceding studies, authors mentioned that the relationship among municipalities differs according to the kind of public services required/offered. Park[2] mentioned that the relationship among municipalities can be classified into "cooperative" and "competitive" and that local governments are competitive in many public service areas. However, as per the results of more detailed analyses, the relationship can be changed according to the respective policy areas. Competitive hypothesis is applicable to the development policy of local areas, while cooperative hypothesis is more suitable for policy areas such as social welfare, education, and public safety.

The applicable models differ in accordance with the scale of municipalities. Soga[3] compared the social-economic model, which focuses on the influence of competition among local governments, and the government system model, which focuses

---

[2] Keeok Park, "Friends and competitors: Policy Interactions between Local Governments in Metropolitan Areas", *Policy Research Quarterly*, vol.50, no.4, 1997.

[3] Soga K., "Municipalities and Social Environment", *Leviathan*, vol.28, 2001, pp.70-96. (Japanese)

on the strength of control from the central government. He found that the applicable model is different according to the scale of local government. In this research, a tradeoff relationship exists between the strength of constraint of movement in a jurisdiction and that of control from the central government. Villages and small towns wherein the strength of constraint of movement is high get more strong control from the central government. In addition, Peterson[4] compared the applicable model for development policy, which greatly influences the economy of the municipality, and the social distribution policy, which badly influences the economy of local government. He found that the central government has the primary relationship with social distribution, while local governments are willing to proceed with development policy.

Hypothesis I-1:

Among various public policies, the more the policy has the characteristics of regional development, the more applicable the internal determinant model becomes. The more the policy has the characteristics of social distribution or social welfare, the more applicable the vertical determinant model is.

Hypothesis I-2:

The regional diffusion model is applicable for all public policies in Japan.

Based on these preceding studies, I analyze Park's discussion, in which applicable models differ in accordance

---

[4] P.E.Peterson, *City Limits*, University of Chicago press,1981.

Factors Regulating Implementation Processes   43

with the kind of public policies implemented. Hypothesis I-1 details the relation with the variation of policies and the internal determinant model (which is more applicable to the regional development policy). Furthermore, the vertical determinant model is more applicable to the social distribution policy because local governments are more willing to proceed with regional development policies than welfare policies.

Hypothesis I-1 is based on the discussion wherein the central government proceeds with social distribution policy, while local governments are willing to establish regional development policy. Hypothesis I-2 is based on an idiosyncratic cultural aspect of the Japanese, which is called "groupism" (group-oriented culture) among local governments and which greatly influences the central government and prefectures in Japan.

Figure 2-2 shows the result of the multiple regression analysis whose independent variables are regional development policy, foundation improvement policy of the daily lives of residents, and social distribution policy. In the analysis, variables of the internal determinant model, regional diffusion model, and vertical determinant model are dependent variables. In detail, "the number of new constructions of public buildings" is the variable of regional development policy, "the number of public parks" is the variable of improvement policy of daily lives, and "the number of elderly people using nursing homes (Institutional) and home help services (Home Help)" is the variable of social distribution policy. Variables of these three models are chosen from the aggregate data of local governments, and the details of the variables used in analysis are

44   **Chapter 2**

◄─────── More Development-Oriented   More Distributive-Oriented ─────►

		Regional Development Policy	Foundation Policy for Residents	Redistributive Policy	
				Institutional	Home Help
A	Increase of population				
	Percentage of elderly				
	Rate of service industry		.249**		
	Gap of population	.143**			
	Elderly with children	.097*			−.226**
	House Possession		.414***		
	Annual Expenditure		.153**	.187**	
	Expenditure for Policy		.137***		
	Public Finance Balance	−.167***			−.127+
	Percentage of Debt		−.103*		
	Past Record of Mayor A				
B	Number of cities				
	Population in area	.277***	.296***		
	Gap of population	.119***	.126*		
	Quantity of service		.242***	.255**	.327**
C	Index of Finance				
	Past Record of Mayor B		.151**	−.101*	
	Central Disbursement			.145*	
	Prefecture Disbursement	−.101*	−.105**	.159**	−.190**
	National Grant				
	R−square	.297	.425	.175	.165
	Number	570	570	565	565

(0≤***<0.005   0.005≤**<0.01   0.01≤*<0.05   0.05≤+0.1)
A: Variables that refer to the internal determinant model
B: Variables that refer to the regional diffusion model
C: Variables that refer to the vertical determinant model

Figure 2-2 Result of Analysis for Hypothesis I

described in the footnote[5]. The number of municipalities for analysis is 640.

---

[5] The way of analysis and variables on Hypothesis 1 is as follows.
(1) Way of analysis: Multiple Regression Analysis
(2) Unit of analysis: 640 cities in 2001.

Factors Regulating Implementation Processes 45

I made the regression model for all the variables described above, but in the figure, only significant variables are described numerically. The significant level is showed by the number of asterisks (*), and the greater the number of asterisks the variable has, the more applicable it is for the model. The

---

(3) Independent Variables:

Regional Development Policy = number of new construction of the buildings

Improvement Policy for daily lives = number of park

Social Redistribution Policy = number of waiting elderly of nursing home

quantity of social welfare services

(4) Dependent Variables:

Internal Determinant Model

Social Environment = Increase of Population, The Aging Rates, Rate of Service Industry、 Gap of Population between Day and Night, Percentage of Working Women, Percentage of Home Possession, Percentage of the Elderly living with their Children

Budgetary Environment = Annual Expenditure per person、 Percentage of Expenditure for the peculiar Policy、 Percentage of Debt

Political Environment = Past Record of Mayor A=Strength of Relation with Social Welfare Policy in past record of mayor (Form Strong=5 to Non=0)

Regional Determinant Model

Each municipality belongs to the special area for policy implementation in Japan. The variables here are all established on the basis of this special area.

Number of cities within the special public area、 Population in the special public area, Gap of population between day and night in special public area, quantity of public services=quantity of a municipality / sum of the quantity of public services implemented in municipalities within the same special public area.

Vertical Determinant Model

Budgetary Relation = Index of Finance, Percentage of National Disbursement within Whole Revenue, Percentage of Prefecture Disbursement within Whole Revenue, Percentage of National Grant within Whole Revenue,

Personal Relation = Past Record of Mayor B=Strength of Relation with Public Administrators in the Central Government (Form Strong=5 to Non=0)

strength of the relationship between the independent variables and dependent variables is shown by the number, and a plus or minus in front of the number indicates the direction of the relation.

According to the result of the analysis, the applicable model differs with the type of public policy. Which model is most applicable for a particular public policy can be understood by the number of applicable variables. Concerning Hypothesis I-1, we can conclude from the results of the regression analysis that variables of the internal determinant model are most applicable for regional development policy. Variables of vertical determinant model are applicable for the social redistribution policy. Therefore, Hypothesis 1-1 can be understood as supportable.

Hypothesis I-2 also can be understood as supportable because variables of the regional determinant model are applicable for most policy areas. However, when examined in detail, these variables proved to be more applicable for the regional development policy and foundation improvement policy for the daily lives of residents, whereas the applicable level is comparatively low for the social redistribution policy. Therefore, concerning the social welfare policy, the focus in this book, the influence of the regional determinant model is considered to be weaker in comparison with those of other policies. Rather, the regional determinant model is more applicable for the regional development types of public policies.

Concerning the social welfare policy for elderly, compared with other policy areas, the vertical determinant model is most applicable and the influence of the regional determinant model is not as strong. Hence, we can conclude that the social welfare policy in municipalities has been decided and implemented by the strong control of the central government to guarantee public services at the national minimum level to all citizens in Japan.

3. BACKGROUND OF THE HYPOTHESIS

The discussion above is fundamentally based on deductive process. I have used two theoretical models introduced in the preceding research and have added one for analyzing Japanese bureaucracy. Therefore, an inductive approach will be needed to clarify the discussion. I consider the background of the models from the research interviews of public officials who take charge of the social welfare for elderly. I check the validity of the three hypotheses by utilizing an inductive approach.

Three municipalities were chosen for interview research in Chiba prefecture for two specific reasons. Chiba Prefecture was chosen from 47 prefectures across Japan because Chiba's character was an epitome of Japan in terms of the structure of its population and industrial infrastructure. It is the most popular prefecture in Japan for interview and questionnaire research. I chose three municipalities from cities and villages in the Chiba Prefecture because these municipalities had almost the same scale and population and were located far from each other. I sent questionnaires to all municipalities in the Chiba Prefecture before this interview research, and from the results of this, I ascertained that these municipalities had the varying types of social services for elderly.

Three municipalities wherein I conducted research interviews had almost the same demographics and played similar roles in each special welfare area. These were middle-class municipalities, and leaders in this particular specialist welfare area. However, despite the similarity in characteristics, public officials assume importance in different ways, i.e., as "social, economic, and political actors within the jurisdiction," via their "relationship among neighboring municipalities," and in their "relationship with the central government and the upper levels of local governments," in their decision making.

Municipality A has about 1.2 million people (as of October 1, 2003) and a generally middle-class demographic. The percentage of elderly among residents is about 15.4%. Because it is located far from the center of the Chiba Prefecture, it has deep relationships with neighboring cities and villages rather than with Chiba City, which is the centre of the Chiba Prefecture. Residents in Municipality A are willing to participate in the policymaking of local governments, and public officials offer public services by following the requirements outlined by residents. The relationship among both neighboring municipalities and between the central government or the upper level of local government does not generally influence the decision making of Municipality A.

Several policies and programs for the elderly are established on the basis of the "Revised Ten-Year Strategy to Promote Health Care and Welfare for the Elderly" (The New Gold Plan) and the "Public Long-Term Care Insurance Project Plan." When these fundamental plans were established, experts on health, medicine, and social welfare established the formal meetings several times. Numerous residents were also able to participate in the meetings to voice their opinions on the policies. To get broader opinions of residents, public officials held explanation meetings several times in community and send many questionnaires to residents. However, public officials did not visit the houses of residents or their villages to get public opinions by themselves. They knew only the opinions of residents who participated in these meetings.

The day service is the most popular service among services within the insurance system. However, people are not willing to use the home help service despite the positive offers of services from public officials. This is a reflection of the consciousness of residents that they do not want to let home helpers get into their houses because they are strangers for them even after the new public long-term care insurance system was established. The mayor of Municipality A has actively tried to improve social welfare policy for elderly, and public officials follow his will. Thus, social services in Municipality A progress speedily not only in public areas but also in the private domain. Many companies are now related not only to providing social welfare programs in the city but also to evaluating the public services. They try to get many opinions and evaluations from the residents by conducting interview research and sending questionnaires. Because the budget of the city is not large, the mayor is not willing to establish more public nursing homes and institutions; instead, the mayor would help companies provide social welfare services. Presently, there are eight nursing homes in the city, but more than 100 elderly persons are waiting for access to these homes.

Municipality B has about 1.2 million people (as of October 1, 2003) and middle-class demographic, and the percentage of elderly among residents is about 16.2%. For a long time, the relationship of residents among the three neighboring cities has been deeply interwoven in their daily lives, and even now, these four cities are cooperative in providing public services across several policy areas. Municipality B is the leader city among neighboring municipalities; in the area of social welfare,

50   Chapter 2

Municipality B is the first city among its four neighbors to have established a nursing home for the elderly. Therefore, for Municipality B, the relationship among the three neighboring municipalities greatly influences the decision-making process of public policy implementation.

Because Municipality B is not wealthy from a budgetary viewpoint, it tries to improve social welfare policies by cooperating with neighbors. Public officials try to improve social welfare policies on the basis of the "Revised Ten-Year Strategy to Promote Health Care and Welfare for the Elderly" (The New Gold Plan) and the "Public Long-Term Care Insurance Project Plan." Municipality B sent questionnaires for residents to ascertain their opinions. When public officials established and reconsidered their policy plans, they opened these meetings to experts. Because Municipality B is the leader of these four cities, it greatly influences the policy implementation process of its three neighboring municipalities. These three cities are positively impacted upon by the leader and have been willing to improve their social welfare institutions accordingly. Because of these good relationships with each other, institutional services for the elderly in these cities have proceeded excellently in comparison with those in other areas. Now, these cities are trying to improve social welfare services in caring for the elderly at home while being cautious in a cooperative way.

Municipality C has about 0.8 million people (as of October 1, 2003) and middle-class demographic, and the percentage of elderly among residents is about 24.5%. Even though the speed of depopulation is not so fast owing to the fisheries and sightseeing, the rate of aging here is fast and is a serious problem for the city. Public officials try to improve social welfare

Factors Regulating Implementation Processes 51

policies on the basis of the "Revised Ten-Year Strategy to Promote Health care and welfare for the Elderly" (The New Gold Plan) and the "Public Long-Term Care Insurance Project Plan." Municipality C sent questionnaires for residents to garner their opinions. When public officials established and reconsidered the plans, they opened these meetings to experts. The city is not so wealthy from a budgetary point of view, and this negatively impacts the ability to improve its social welfare services.

Because of these budgetary constraints, Municipality C essentially follows the policy of the central government and prefectures to get as much national aid as possible. Public officials improve only programs that can receive national aid, and they are also not willing to cooperate with neighboring municipalities. Although public officials in Municipality C also try to ascertain public opinion as much as possible, the impact of the opinion of residents is not so great. Officials have little choice but to follow the decision of the center to get national grants.

Here, I compare the background of the policy processes of these three municipalities. Concerning Municipality B, its history greatly influences it even with regard to the current policy process mechanisms. For a long time, the southern area of the Chiba Prefecture, which contains Municipality B and its neighboring cities, has cooperated with each other in offering public services because relationships among neighbors in these communities are deeply woven in the daily lives of residents. Citizens of this area are not so active in participating in the decision making of public policy. Rather, people are getting used to being passive toward public officials. In the north area of Chiba Prefecture including Municipality A, cities are not so

Table 2-1 Comparison among three municipalities

	Municipality A	Municipality B	Municipality C
Scale of Jurisdiction	Middle	Middle	Middle
Leadership	High	High	High
Characteristics of Municipalities	• Urbanized Area • Positive Participation of Residents • Budget Constrain	• Cooperation with Neighbors • Passive Residents • Budget Constrain	• Fisheries and Sightseeing • Not Cooperative with Residents • Budget Constrain
Priority of Policies	• In-Home Services (especially Day Service) • Precautions	• In-Home Services • Precautions • Urgent Report Network System	• Network System for In-home Services • Precautions
Ways for Getting Public Opinion	• Committee with Experts and Residents • Questionnaires • Direct Petition for Mayor	• Committee with Experts and Residents • Questionnaires	• Committee with Experts and Residents • Questionnaires
Main Factors Influencing Policy Process	• Progressiveness of Mayor to Welfare • Positive Participation of Residents	• Cooperation with Neighboring Municipalities	• Following the Center to get National Grants
Applicable Model	The Internal Determinant Model	The Regional Diffusion Model	The Vertical Determinant Model

Factors Regulating Implementation Processes 53

cooperative with others because of the active participation of residents within their own jurisdiction. Rather than cooperating with other cities or following decisions of the center, cities in this area try to establish their own original plans and policies that fit their area's public needs. In the coastal area including Municipality C, in contrast, there are several small towns and villages, and Municipality C does not have the neighboring municipalities that have such similar characteristics. Thus, Municipality C is not willing to cooperate with municipalities around it. Citizens of this area are also not so willing to participate in the policy process. Thus, Municipality C tries to follow the decision of the center. By doing so, public officials do not have to struggle hard to get a feel for public opinion and can also obtain national grants.

The results of the research interviews are shown in **Table 2-1**. Accordingly, we can conclude that these three models, the internal determinant model, regional diffusion model, and vertical determinant model, are all valid results of this research. The main factors regulating these models are historical aspects, citizen's attitudes toward public policy, and budgetary conditions of these municipalities.

CHAPTER 3

POLICY PROCESS AND CHARACTERISTICS

Preceding analysis showed us the fact that social welfare policy for the elderly in Japan was established and implemented on the basis of the Vertical Determinant Model. However, because social policy for the elderly contains many kinds of policies and programs, we should analyze in more detail policy process and the characteristics of these variety of policies and programs in order to make sure whether applicable models for analyzing the policy process are different depending on the policies and programs. In other words, by focusing on the many different programs in same policy area, social welfare policy for the elderly, I would like to analyze the relationship between the applicable models and characteristics of the policies produced by.

1. DEVELOPMENT OF SOCIAL WELFARE POLICY IN JAPAN

Aging in Japan is accelerating at a fast pace that no other developed nations have experienced before. The aging rate already reached 16.2% in 1998, and one in every six persons of the total population is 65 years old or older. According to the population estimate for the future, one in four persons will

Policy Process and Characteristics 55

be age 65 old or older in around 2020, and the aging rate will be about 25% thereby reaching the world's highest level[1].

The progress of welfare for the elderly has been a history of our efforts to meet the growing demands for welfare for the elderly with the advancement of aging. Before the enforcement of the Welfare Law for the elderly in 1963, welfare for the elderly was clearly written limited to a very small number of people with low income, and those elderly people were housed in nursing facilities for the elderly in accordance with the Public Assistant Law. For a long time, living with multiple generations in a household has been a common practice in Japan and the care for the elderly has been considered as a responsibility of the family. However, the approaches toward care for elderly parents have gradually changed along with the changes in the family system, family succession, as well as the consequences of industrialization, and also with the increase of non-traditional family forms emerging as a result of population being concentrated into metropolitan areas.

Upon the establishment of the Welfare Law for the elderly, physical checkups were implemented and the system for special nursing homes for the elderly was established to admit any elderly people requiring long-term care without limiting it to the elderly people with low income. Also, the home helper system for the elderly-only households (current home-visit care) was institutionalized and the measures have become available to all elderly people who need special support. Systematic and comprehensive promotions of such measures

---

[1] The description of this section is based on the Annual Report on Health and Welfare 1999 officially published by the Ministry of Health, Labor and Welfare.

started to improve welfare for all elderly people. However, when the Welfare Law for the elderly was enforced, the actual scope of welfare serviced users were limited to the elderly with low income, as observed in the facts that most welfare facilities for the elderly were nursing homes for elderly people with low income or indigents, and the subjects for the home helper dispatch system were limited to the elderly with low incomes.

Welfare services for the elderly have become available to general elderly people following the 1980s when the demands for welfare for the elderly increased rapidly with the extension of life expectancy, expansion of the aging population, and a remarkable increase of elderly-only households.

Over more than 50 since the end of WW2, the Social Welfare System has shown diversifying expansion and changes. Particularly, the following changes are observed in the overall roles of welfare services.

A. Centralization of welfare services

The characteristics of welfare services are changing from special and selective services for the poor to more general and universal services available to anybody who needs the services regardless of their income.

B. User-oriented mechanisms and improved service quality

The mechanisms for using the services is changing from the system that sees the administrative offices decide and provide certain services to a user-oriented system where users can select and use the services based on their decision. More specifically, the system is changing form a fixed system to a user contract system, and also the discussion on the mechanism to support service users such as protection for people's rights and disclosure of information has likewise begun. In addition, the requests for changing from a fixed service to diversified high quality services are increasing to meet individual needs.

C. Municipality centered mechanisms

In order to provide detailed services to meet the needs of local people, the service mechanisms are shifting to being more municipality centered. Under the conventional system, a municipality was processing administrative work for welfare as commissioned by the National Agency, but during 1980's it was commissioned by a service organization, and them in 1990 with the revision of welfare system, municipalities were authorized to take leadership in improving the welfare of residents including welfare for the elderly and for the people with physical disabilities. It has become important for municipalities to lead the improvement efforts for local welfare to meet the needs in their own communities.

The medical care and pensions were the core items of the measures for the elderly during 1970's to 1980's, including the improvement of pension benefits, increase of medical insurance benefit ratio, free medical services to the elderly and the establishment of a health service system for the elderly. Then, actions for improved welfare services and long-term care became important issues in late 1980s. Considering the support for families with elderly people requiring long-term

58   Chapter 3

Table 3-1 Overview of Social Welfare Policy for the Elderly

Relevant Laws	Welfare Law for the elderly (established in 1963)
Number of Subjects	1,825 per 10,000 people
Welfare Facilities	Special nursing homes for the elderly (3,713 locations)
	Day service centers for the elderly (5,625 locations)
	Short-stay facilities for the elderly (33 locations)
	Support centers for long-term care (3,570 centers)
In-home Services	Support for elderly people's living at home
	• In-home care for the elderly
	• Day service for the elderly
	• Short-stay for the elderly
Other Programs	• Precautions
	• Special Programs for more wealthy lives of the elderly

(Development of basic foundation through the promotion of the Gold Plan)

care, the need for improved In-home services was emphasized. As a result, short-term care (short stay) services and daily commuting care services (day services) were institutionalized and the number of home-visit care-givers (home helpers) was increased.

In 1990 when eight welfare related laws including the Welfare Law for the elderly were revised, the administrative work for the admission of the elderly and people with disabilities was transferred to municipal offices from prefectural offices (Cities had already had such responsibilities). With this change both In-home welfare services and welfare for the elderly and disabled came under the management of the municipality in question. With this, all prefectures and municipalities

Policy Process and Characteristics   **59**

Table 3-2 Overview of the Gold Plan and the New Gold Plan

Relevant Policy	"Ten-Year Strategy to Promote Health Care and Welfare for the Elderly" (The Gold Plan) (Established in December 1898) "Review of Ten-Year Strategy to Promote Health Care and Welfare for the Elderly" (The New Gold Plan) (in December 1994)
Basic Concept	In order to realize a society in which all elderly people, including those with mental or physical disabilities, can maintain their dignity and live a self-sufficient life, we shall construct a system that makes long-term care services which are necessary for self-sufficiency easily accessible to all who need them, as long-term care needs represent the greatest concern in the post retirement life of most people. 1. User-orientation and self-sufficiency support 2. Universalism 3. Provision of comprehensive services 4. Localism

Goals for the end of 1999		
1. In-home services		
(1) Home helpers	170,000 people	
(2) Short-Stay	for 60,000 people	
(3) Day service / Day care	17, 000 facilities	
(4) In-home care support centers	10,000 centers	
2. Facility services		
(1) Special nursing homes for the elderly	for 290,000 people	
(2) Health services facilities for the elderly	for 280,000 people	
(3) Multipurpose senior centers	400 centers	
(4) Care houses	for 100,000 people	
3. Training and securing manpower		
(1) Matrons, long-term care staff	200,000 people	
(2) Nursing personnel, etc.	100,000 people	
(3) Occupational / Physical therapists	15,000 people	

(Plans for health and welfare services for the elderly and long-term care insurance) were then assigned the responsibility of developing plans for health and welfare for the elderly and setting target values for the development of various services by the end of fiscal year 1999. This was in order to promote a comprehensive and systematic implementation of health and welfare services for the elderly and completed the development of their plans.

The establishment of the mechanisms for municipalities to lead the implementation of health and welfare services for elderly people was a significant change. Currently, more than 10% of total municipalities in Japan have already exceeded the aging rate of 30%. Including urban areas, the improvement of health and welfare measures for elderly people has already been a top-ranking request from residents to the local administrative offices.

The public long-term care insurance system, effective from April 2000, will further emphasize the importance of the role played by municipalities. The public long-term care insurance system has been developed by totally reorganizing the current welfare system for the elderly in combination with the medical services for elderly people requiring care, and aims to offer a large part of conventional welfare services for the elderly through the mechanism of social insurance. Municipalities are positioned as the insurers that operate the public long-term care insurance system, and they are expected to exercise leadership in creating business plans for the long-term care insurance and developing infrastructure for long-term care services based on the plans. Their responsibilities also include creating a community in which residents can live with sense of security by resolving their concerns about long-term care through the administrative work to certify the long-term care needs, management of insured persons, the handling of insurance benefits, etc.

2. ANALYSIS OF INDEPENDENT VARIABLES

Before we begin the main analysis of this chapter, I would like to consider the difference of characteristics among many programs in the same policy area, namely, social welfare policy for the elderly. By doing so, we will be able to see the present situation of the policy implementation in municipalities and also the prospect of whether the model applicable for the analysis of the policy process will be different owing to the difference of the characteristics of programs.

There are a lot of different programs which contain aspects of the social welfare policy for the elderly, and we have to consider two aspects of policies for analyzing these programs. One aspect is "the difference of quantity" of the policy, and the other is that of "quality." Quantity is easier for us to study because it is visible and we can use aggregate data for comparing the quantity of services among municipalities. Frequency of use of In-home care services and numbers of beds in nursing homes are the typical aggregate data in this policy area used in comparing the quantity of services among municipalities. On the other hand, assessing quality of service is more difficult for us to analyze, because it is not visible and we cannot get accurate information of quality only by examining aggregate data. The degree of satisfaction with the policy is obtained via the typical data for considering quality, and survey data is more usable for this kind of study. Concerning the quantity data, which I shall mainly be using in this book, there will be two kinds of data. One is the data on the programs that most municipalities have, and concerning these kinds of services, the quality of the services can be analyzed by the frequency of use or number of institutions. The other is the data on the programs that some municipalities have and some do not, so whether the municipalities have the program can indicate the data on the difference of quantity.

I will mainly use the quantity data in this book and try to consider two kinds of programs described above. Concerning the data through which we can study the quantity via the comparison of frequency of use or numbers of institutions, I would like to use three different programs, i.e., home-visit care services, day services, and short-stay services for In-home services, and two programs, i.e., special nursing homes for the elderly and support centers for long-term care for welfare facility services. On the other hand, concerning the data on whether the municipalities have these kinds of programs or not, it can be the raw data itself, and I would like to examine four kinds of programs on precautions for caring and support services for a useful life in municipalities.

The difference of quantity on the three kinds of In-home services, home-visit services, day services, and short-stay services, is described in **Figure 3-1**. The difference is shown by prefectures, and we can understand that the difference among prefectures is largest regarding the home-visit service, while it is smallest regarding the short-stay service. Quantity of service is higher in Western areas, while lower in Eastern areas on day services. Considering the details, frequency of usage is high in prefectures, such as Chiba, Yamanashi, Tottori, and Miyagi, while it is lower in prefectures, such as Tokyo, Hyogo, and Fukuoka.

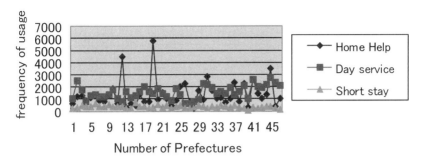

Figure 3-1 Frequency of Usage: In-Home Services

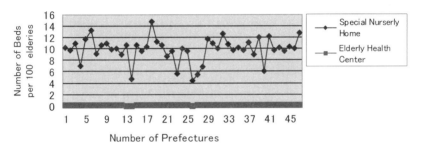

Figure 3-2 Number of beds per elderly in Welfare Institutions

The difference of quantity regarding two kinds of services, special nursing homes for the elderly and health service facilities for the elderly, is described in **Figure 3-2**. The difference is shown as the number of beds in institutions per 100 elderly who need care by prefectures, and we can understand that the difference of special nursing homes among prefectures is larger than that of health service facilities. Considering the detail, number of beds per 100 elderly who need care in institutions is high in prefectures, such as Yamagata, Fukui, Shizuoka, Mie, Nara, Shimane, Kochi, Saga, and Okinawa, while it is low in prefectures, such as Miyagi, Aichi, Kyoto, and Fukuoka.

We can know from these figures that there are two kinds of sub- policies being implemented via the same social welfare policy, and one is that the difference of quantity is large among prefectures, whereas the other is very small. Because of the characteristics of analysis in this chapter, I would like to use the data of programs whose quantity is quite different among the areas selected for analysis. Therefore, I will choose frequency of usage of the home help service as the representative of In-home services, and number of beds in special nursing home for 100 elderly who need care as the representative for welfare institution services.

As I have noted, there are two kinds of services in social welfare policy affecting the elderly in Japan. One is services which are included in the long-term care insurance system and the other is those outside the insurance system. **Table 3-3** shows the variety of programs conducted as precautions and special programs for wealthy life for the elderly in Yamaguchi Prefecture, and each municipality picks up form these programs for implementation within its jurisdiction. Because these services outside the insurance system are also analyzed in this book, I will choose four programs from these services for analysis which have different characteristics as much as possible when making comparisons (see **Table 3-4**). Concerning the services within the insurance system, because all prefectures and municipalities are implementing the same kinds of services, that is home-visit services, day services, short-stay services, special nursing homes, and health service facilities, I would like to use the frequency of usage and number of beds per 100 elderly who need care for the independent variables. On the other hand, concerning the variables outside the insurance system, because each prefecture and municipality chose the programs from among many for their implementation, whether the municipality has the program or not can be used

Table 3-3 Examples of Precautions and Special Programs

(in Yamaguchi Prefecture, 2004)

Special Programs for Precautions and Wealthy Living for the elderly

City Number	Name of Cities	Meal Delivery	Help for Going out	Cleaning Beds	Home Visit	Home Repairs	Hair Cut	Short Stay
35201	Shimonoseki	✓	✓		✓	✓	✓	✓
35202	Ube	✓			✓	✓		✓
35203	Yamaguchi	✓	✓	✓	✓	✓		✓
35204	Hagi	✓	✓	✓	✓	✓	✓	✓
35205	Tokuyama	✓		✓	✓	✓		✓
35206	Houfu	✓	✓	✓	✓	✓	✓	✓
35207	Kudamatsu	✓	✓	✓	✓	✓	✓	✓
35208	Iwakuni	✓		✓	✓	✓		✓
35209	Onoda	✓	✓	✓	✓	✓	✓	✓
35210	Hikari	✓	✓	✓	✓	✓	✓	✓
35211	Nagato	✓		✓	✓	✓	✓	✓

(Omit Below)

Table 3-4 Independent Variables on Precautions and Special Programs

Names of Programs (Independent Variables)	Characteristics of Programs
Repair of Homes	Programs for helping the elderly to repair their homes.
Urgent System	Programs to establish Urgent Information Network System.
Help for going out	Programs for helping the elderly to go to welfare facilities.
Precautions	Programs for precautions and more wealthy living.

Note: 1/0 variables are used as independent variables.
Number 1=The municipality has the program
Number 0=The municipality does not have the program

as the independent variable. The characteristics of programs which I chose for analysis of services outside the insurance system are shown in **Table 3-4**.

3. POLICY PROCESS AND HYPOTHESES

In next section, I will consider the policy process of social welfare for the elderly in more detail and would like to discuss the relationship between the policy process and three hypotheses. In other words, I will discuss how these three models, the Vertical Determinant Model, which is described A in **Figure 3-3**, the Internal Determinant Model, which is described B in the figure, and the Regional Diffusion Model, which is described C in the figure, are related to each other.

In Figure 3-3, the policy process, from the establishment of basic policy by the central government to the implementation by municipalities in each jurisdiction, is shown as part of the social welfare policy for the elderly in Japan. As is shown

Policy Process and Characteristics

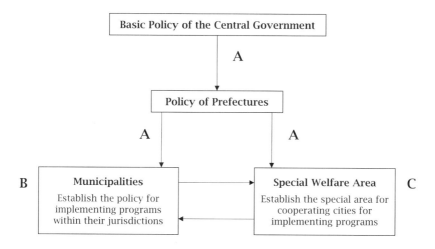

A: The Vertical Determinant Policy Process
B: The Internal Determinant Policy Process
C: The Regional Diffusion Policy Process

Figure 3-3 Policy Process of Social Welfare in Japan

in the figure, social welfare policy has the policy process where, basically, the central government establishes the fundamental policy and the upper level of local government, prefectures, established sub-policy for implementation, and municipalities implement them by adjusting them within their jurisdictions. Under the policy in the era of the Gold Plan, the central government established the fundamental policy of social welfare for the elderly, and each prefecture made a similar Gold Plan for implementation in each jurisdiction by following the main plan of the central government. Even after the system has been basically changed to the long-term care insurance system, the mechanism of the decision-making process is not changed dramatically, and that is why the Vertical Determinant Policy Process still exists in the chart.

68 Chapter 3

After this first process, each municipality establishes their own Gold Plan which includes the concrete implementation plan of both In-home services and welfare facility services by following the plan of prefectures through several research studies of residents. Both A (Vertical Determinant Model) and B (Internal Determinant Model) are applicable for this second process, because not only do municipalities fundamentally follow the policy of the central government and prefectures, they also have to make their original plans by getting information from residents. In addition, there is often the case that several municipalities cooperate with each other for making their plans by establishing a Special Welfare Cooperation Area, process of which can be described by C (Regional Diffusion Model) in the figure.

Figure 3-4 describes the policy process in each municipality, from the establishment of the policy based on several research studies of residents, to the implementation within each jurisdiction. Firstly, each municipality tries to grasp the needs of residents for the policy by doing several kinds of research. It also considers the record of usage in the previous year and establishes the standards of each service for their implementation. This process can be understood as B (Internal Determinant Model), because policy is established on the basis of conditions and needs of residents. After each municipality finished defining the respective standards of each service, the implementation process is deeply related to the policy of the central government and prefectures, and this can be understood as A (Vertical Determinant Model). Also, in the concrete implementation process, municipalities cooperate with each other for more efficient implementation, which process will be represented by C (Regional Diffusion Model). Therefore,

Policy Process and Characteristics 69

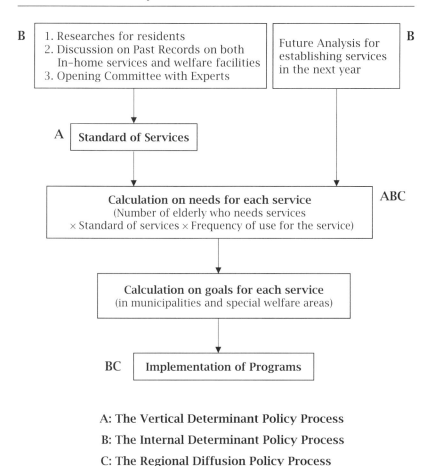

A: The Vertical Determinant Policy Process
B: The Internal Determinant Policy Process
C: The Regional Diffusion Policy Process

Figure 3-4 Policy Process of Social Welfare in Japan

each of these three models are deeply related to the establishment of policy in municipalities. In concrete implementation, B (Internal Determinant Model) and C (Regional Diffusion Model) are basically applicable while A (Vertical Determinant Model) is not so influential with regards to the implementation process.

In this section, I discussed the relationship between policy process and three models, and found that all three models, the Vertical Determinant Model, the Internal Determinant Model,

70 Chapter 3

and the Regional Diffusion Model, are related to each level of policy process, but the strength of the relation is different up to the level of policy process. Therefore, in next session, I would like to focus on the strength of relations between and analyze the policy process in more detail.

4. HYPOTHESES AND CHARACTERISTICS CONCERNING THE POLICY

In Japan, because social welfare policy for elderly was forced introduced by the great leadership of the central government in the era of Gold Plan, there is not so much difference among municipalities in terms of variety of services implemented in each city, and the period that these services were firstly introduced. In other words, all the prefectures and municipalities have the same kind of programs, namely, home-visit services, day services, short-stay services for In-home services, and special nursing homes and health care facilities for welfare facilities for elderly. Also, these programs were introduced in the similar time by following the policy of the central government, and almost all prefectures and municipalities firstly introduced these services for the same reasons[2].

As I described before, social welfare for elderly in Japan is roughly classified into two groups. One is the programs

---

[2] Strictly, some proceeding municipalities began the programs before the central government established the policy, and in these municipalities, there was a variety of reasons for starting programs earlier than the central government. However, because these proceeding municipalities are very few, I would like to omit them from the analysis in order to simplify the discussion.

Policy Process and Characteristics

within the long-term care insurance system and the other is the programs outside the insurance system. There is usually a distinction between which departments take charge of these two kinds of programs, but in small municipalities, the same public staff take charge of both kinds of programs. In either case, the characteristics of the two kinds of programs are fundamentally different, but some parts of the program overlap between municipalities.

Because the kind of programs and the standards for implementation are basically established by the central government concerning the programs within the insurance system, the quantity of services implemented in the municipalities, such as frequency of use by residents, or number of beds in institutions per 100 elderly who need care, is the main focus of the analysis. On the other hand, concerning the programs outside the insurance system, each municipality picks up some programs from among many which are established by the central government. Therefore, whether a particular program is implemented or not is the main focus of the analysis, because municipalities choose particular programs by considering many conditions, such as the budget constrain and needs of residents for programs.

Concerning the programs in the insurance system, some programs have almost full usage by residents, such as special nursing homes for the elderly, while other programs do not have enough usage by residents, such as home help services. Programs outside the insurance system can also be classified into two groups: one is the programs which are fundamentally related to the physical aspect of the system the elderly, and the other is basically related to the mental health aspect of care for the elderly.

Here, I would like to focus on the social welfare policy for the elderly which is classified into the redistribution policy, and try to analyze programs therein. Concretely, I will make sure the fact that different models can be applicable for different programs owing to the characteristics of them by using the three models I described before. As the result of the analysis on HypothesisI-1, the Vertical Determinant Model is more applicable than the Internal Determinant Model and the Regional Determinant Model for social welfare policy for the elderly whose primary characteristic is redistributive. However, because there are many programs with different characteristics (even in social welfare policy), I would like to analyze them in more detail in this section. The hypotheses for analysis are as follows.

Hypothesis II-1:

Among many programs in the social welfare policy for the elderly, the Vertical Determinant Model is more applicable for the programs which help daily lives of the elderly physically, while the Internal Determinant Model is more applicable for the programs which support the mental health aspect of the elderly.

Hypothesis II-2:

The Regional Determinant Model is applicable for all the programs in social welfare policy for the elderly.

Four different types of independent variables are used in analyses on the basis of the characteristics of programs. I chose four variables from aggregate data in four different classifications of the policy, home-visit services and special nursing homes for the elderly among programs in the insurance

Policy Process and Characteristics   73

system, and a program related to the physical aspect of the elderly and that in relation to the mental aspect of elderly care among programs outside the insurance system, all of which are described in **Table 3-5**. The dependent variables used for the analysis are the same as for analyzing Hypothesis I-1 and Hypothesis I-2.

Figure 3-5 is the result of the Multiple Regression Analysis, whose independent variables are described in Table3-4, and dependent variables are aggregate data related to three models[3].

---

[3] The means of analysis and variables used concerning Hypothesis 2-1 and Hypothesis 2-2 are as follows.

Ways of analysis: Multiple Regression Analysis

Unit of analysis: Municipalities (year 2001)

There are about 3,000 municipalities in Japan, and among them, I used the data concerning 900 municipalities which provided data in a perfect way for this particular analysis. The final number of municipalities used for analysis is 859 for programs in the insurance system, and 932 for programs out of the insurance system.

Target of analysis (Independent variables):
1. Frequency of use for home help services by residents.
2. Number of beds per 100 care needing elderly in nursing homes.
3. Whether the municipality has the program helping the elderly going out or not.
4. Whether the municipality has the program of precautions or not.

Dependent Variables:

Increase of the elderly, Rate of the elderly who need care among all the elderly, Rate of service industry, Gross Expenditure per person, Expenditure for social welfare per person, Growth Rate of Revenue per person, Percentage of the elderly living with their children, Rate of working women among all women, Percentage of elderly who possess their own houses, Positive attitude of mayor for social welfare (form Strong =5 to Non=0), Past Record of Mayor A=How strong the mayor has the past record related to the social welfare (form Strong =5 to Non=0)

Number of Cities in special welfare area, Population in special welfare area, Population Gap between day and night, Quantity of Service in the Municipality / Sum of Quantity in Municipalities in the Same Special Welfare Area.

74   Chapter 3

Table 3-5 Independent Variables for the Analysis on Hypothesis II

Independent Variables		Explanation of variables
Programs in the insurance system	Quantity of Usage of In-home Services	Frequency of use of home-visit service in each municipality per 100 elderly who need care
	Quantity of Use of Welfare Institutions	Number of beds in special nursing home for elderly in each municipality per 100 elderly who need care
Programs out of the insurance system	Programs related to the physical aspect	• Program for helping elderly to go out • Programs for helping elderly to repair home
	Programs related the mental aspect	• Urgent Information Network Programs • Precautions and Special Programs

Considering the results of analysis in Figure 3-5, Hypothesis II-1 can be understood to be almost supported. The Vertical Determinant Model is more influential upon the programs which have the characteristics of helping fundamental lives of the elderly, and the Internal Determinant Model is more influential upon the programs which are related to the daily satisfaction levels for lives of the elderly. In addition, considering the variables which characterized the Vertical Determinant

Index of Finance of Municipalities, Past Record B=Strength of Relation with Public Administrators in the Central Government (Form Strong=5 to Non=0), Past Record C=Strength of Relation with Public Officials in Local Government (Form Strong=5 to Non=0), Percentage of Central Disbursement in whole Revenue, Percentage of Prefecture Disbursement in whole Revenue, Percentage of Regular Allocation Tax in whole Revenue, Percentage of Special Allocation Tax in whole Revenue, Accomplish Rate of the Gold Plan.

Policy Process and Characteristics

◄──────── Support for daily lives   Satisfy more wealthy lives ────────►

		Programs in Insurance System		Programs out of Insurance System	
		Special Nursing Home	Home-visit Service	Help of Going out	Precautions
A	Increase of elderly		−.122*	.190*	
	Rate elderly need care	−.293**	−.208***		
	Rate of service industry			−.125*	.133**
	Expenditure per person	.433**			
	Expenditure for welfare		.148**		.133**
	Growth of Revenue	−.153**			.092*
	Elderly with children	.168**		−.101*	
	Rate of working women		.117**	−.048*	
	House possession		−.115*		
	Attitude for welfare			.152**	.396***
	Past Record of Mayor A			−.257**	.106**
B	Number of Cities		.109**	.127*	.413**
	Population in Area			.111*	
	Population Gap				
	Quantity of Service		.523**	.534**	.665**
C	Index of Finance	−.290**			
	Past Record of Mayor B	−.158*			
	Past Record of Mayor C			−.102**	−.147**
	Central Disbursement	−.119**	−.141**		
	Pref. Disbursement				−.108**
	Regular Allocation Tax	.554**			
	Special Allocation Tax	−.408**	−.188*		
	Accomplish Rate	.114**	−.222*		
	R-Square	.470	.339	.236	.344
	Number	559	675	656	656

(0≤*** <0.005 0.005≤** <0.01 0.01≤* <0.05 0.05≤+<0.1)
A: Variables which mean the Internal Determinant Model
B: Variables which mean the Regional Diffusion Model
C: Variables which mean the Vertical Determinant Model

Figure 3-5 Result of Analysis on Hypothesis II

Model in detail, variables on budget constraints are more influential upon the programs which support basic lives of the elderly, while variables on politics are more influential to the programs which help to satisfy more wealthy lives of the elderly. In other words, the programs which support physical aspects of the elderly tend to be decided by the variables related to the needs of residents for the policy, such as the percentage of the elderly living with their children, that of the elderly having their own houses, that of working women, the enthusiastic pursual by the mayor of the social welfare policy, and the programs which help the mental health aspects of elderly care tend to be regulated by the variables related to the strength of relation between the central government and budget constraints.

Hypothesis II-2 can be understood as supportable for the programs whose characteristics are related to the satisfaction of wealthy lives of the elderly and not supportable for the programs related to the physical aspects care for the elderly. In other words, the Regional Diffusion Model is more applicable for the policies which are related to the programs for the overall mental satisfaction of elderly.

Multiple Regression Analysis, which I described above, is suitable for the comparison among variables in the same model. Therefore, it is possible to compare the strength *between* the variables and models, but difficult to compare the effectiveness *among* models. In other words, we cannot figure out the possibility that there are relationships among the models or variables in a step by step fashion. Therefore, in **Figure 3-6** and **Figure 3-7**, I performed a Covariance Structure Analysis by using the same models and variables for the Multiple Regression Analysis in order to clarify the relationship among three models. Here I used the "frequency of use of home-visit services by residents," and the "number of beds in special nursing homes per 100 elderly who need care" as the independent variables, and also used the same dependent variables as in the former analysis.

Concerning the analysis of In-home services, the model began from the variable of the service industry, which has the nature of the structure of industry and the last variable of this

Policy Process and Characteristics 77

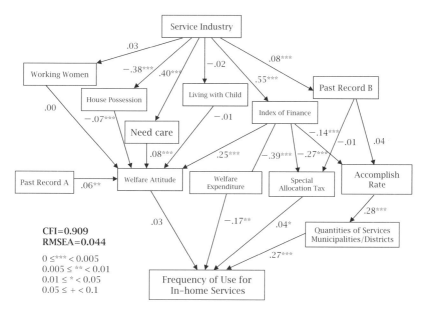

Figure 3-6 The Covariance Structure Analysis on In-home services

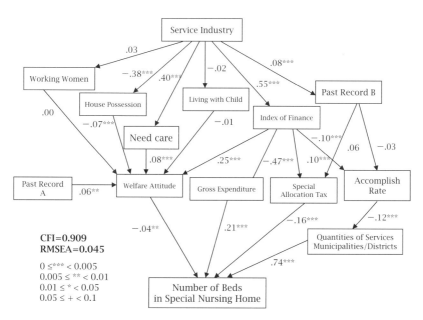

Figure 3-7 The Covariance Structure Analysis on Welfare Facilities

model is the frequency of use for home help services used by residents. The needs required by residents for the policy is shown by variables, such as, percentage of working women, that of home possession, that of the elderly who need care, that of the elderly living with their children, and which are integrated through the usual political routes.

However, the results show that concerning the home-visit services, the impact of the positive attitude of the mayor toward social welfare policy is much smaller than those of the much more tangible reality of budget constraints or the primarily dominant relationship with the central government. In other words, as I mentioned before, not only in the results of the Multiple Regression Analysis, but also in those of the Covariance Structure Analysis, the frequency of use by residents is greatly influenced by budget constraints (the Index of Finance, Total Expenditure for the social welfare per person, Percentage of Special Allocation Tax in whole revenue), the strength of relationship between the central government in political (Past Record of Mayor, Accomplishment Rate of the Gold Plan, Quantity of Service in Special Welfare Area), the typical variable which show the Regional Determinant Model, is also greatly influential to the frequency of use for the services.

Concerning the welfare facilities for the elderly, the model also starts from the variables on the industrial structure, and ends with the independent variable, which is the number beds in institutions per 100 elderly who need care. The tendency of the model for welfare facilities is very similar to that of In-home services, and the impact of the needs of residents for the policy, which is shown through the political route, is much smaller than that of budget constraints or the strength of relation with the central government. Quantity of Service in Special Welfare Areas, the typical variable which shows the Regional Determinant Model, is also greatly influential upon the frequency of use of the service, and from this result, we can conclude that not only the quantity of In-home services, but also that of welfare facilities, are greatly impacted upon by the Vertical Determinant Model and the Regional Diffusion Model.

CHAPTER 4
QUALITY OF POLICY AND THREE MODELS

From several results of the former analyses, we can know that social welfare policies for the elderly are fundamentally brought about by three kinds of policy process, which are described as three models in this book. The strength of the influence of these models relative to the quantity of services is different depending on the difference of nature of the policies and programs, or of the environment among municipalities. The next problem which we have to tackle is clarifying the relationship between the "quality" of policy and the three models. In other words, we must clarify *how* the difference of policy process is related to the *quality* of policy. Which policy process, or model, will be able to bring about the policy which produces the highest satisfaction among residents? In this chapter, I would like to analyze the relation between the policy process and its subsequent performance in order to consider the best way for Japan to establish the ideal policy process of social welfare policy for the elderly.

1. EXAMINING THE VERTICAL DETERMINANT MODEL

As I described in a former chapter, the Vertical Determinant Model can be classified into two groups. One is the Voluntary Vertical Determinant Model, in which public officials in local government follow the policy of the central government to get some merits from the center or to avoid any demerits. The other is the Compulsory Vertical Determinant Model, in which public officials in local governments have to follow the intentions of the central government against their will because of the system of decision-making, such as strict laws, financial aids, and regulations. The main difference between these two models is "whether public officials in local governments intend to follow the policy of the central government." In this session, I would like to clarify which types of the Vertical Determinant Model are more suitable for Japanese bureaucracy, and try to consider what kind of policy will be needed for Japanese society to establish the ideal policy process.

(3)-1: Voluntary Vertical Determinant Model
Public Officials in municipalities follow the intention of the central government or the prefectures to get some merits from the center or to avoid any demerits.

(3)-2: Compulsory Vertical Determinant Model
Public Officials in local governments have to follow the intention of the central government against their will because of the system of decision-making, such as strict laws, financial aids, and regulations.

In order to clarify which types of the model are more applicable for the Japanese policy making process, I sent questionnaires to public officials in all municipalities and prefectures who take charge of the social welfare policy for the elderly within their jurisdictions. In this research, public officials answer the four types of questions: Strength of application and the concrete example of the Vertical Determinant Model; Strength of application and the concrete example of the Internal Determinant Model; Strength of application and the concrete example of the Regional Diffusion Model; Which model do you think will be most applicable for the concrete policy process in your jurisdiction?

The main object of this research is to clarify the most applicable model, and if it is the Vertical Determinant Model, which type of the model is more suitable for the status quo?

The questionnaires were mailed to the public officials in 47 prefectures and 640 cities during the summer of 2003. The percentage of collecting questionnaires is about 57.45 % (27 letters) for prefectures and 60.25% (401 letters) for cities. The sum of the percentage of collecting questionnaires is 62.23% (428 letters) and the content of the questionnaires are described in each figure.

Concerning the question on the Internal Determinant Model, the answers are classified into nine groups. The smaller the number is, the more general way of getting needs of residents, and the bigger the number is, the more original the way of ascertaining the needs through many dialogs. The result of the research on this question is in **Figure 4-1**.

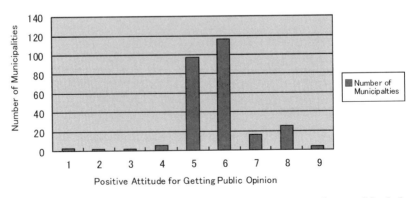

Figure 4-1 The result on the Internal Determinant Model

Q1. Question on the Internal Determinant Model

What kind of way do you use mostly for getting the public opinion on the period of introducing new policies or revising the existing policies?

(Multiple answers are possible)

1. Public officials do nothing in particular to get the information from the residents, but decide the policy by following the guidelines and standards of the central government.

2. Public officials guess the needs of residents by statistical calculation of data from research.

3. Professionals within social welfare establish the policy, and public officials explain it to the residents.

4. Public officials decide the concrete policy through direct contact with the public and private institutions that provide social welfare services.

5. The committee organized by professionals, public officials, and ambassadors of residents establish the policy.

6. Public officials do several kinds of research with the residents and institutions which provide social welfare services, and establish the most appropriate policy following the results of this.

7. Public officials take direct contact to the informal groups of residents within the community and establish the policy on the basis of the information and opinion from them.

8. Public officials directly visit the community and obtain public opinion.

9. Public officials directly visit the homes of users of the services and get information.

Chapter 4

The results show that most municipalities either use questionnaires or open the professional committee for getting information and public opinion. In some proceeding cities, public officials directly visit the user's home in order to ascertain opinion or take direct contact to informal groups within the community, but most municipalities still garner public opinion through indirect means. Only some proceeding cities try to make direct contact with residents themselves.

Next, concerning the question on the Regional Diffusion Model, answers can be classified into five groups on the basis of the strength of relationships among neighboring municipalities. As the number becomes smaller, the relationship is weaker. In other words, as the number is bigger, the relationship is stronger, and in the strong relation, municipalities cooperate with neighbors, not only in the establishment of the policy, but also in its implementation. The result of the question is **Figure 4-2**.

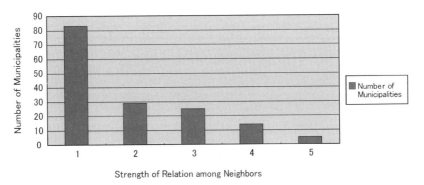

Figure 4-2 The result on the Regional Diffusion Model

Q2. Questions on the Regional Diffusion Model

How strong is the relationship among the neighboring municipalities in the establishment and implementation of the social welfare policy for elderly?

(Choose one from five choices)

1. There is almost no relationship among neighbors or is only the regular meeting in order to exchange information.
2. Public officials cooperate together for studying and researching the policy.
3. Public officials in plural municipalities visit proceeding cities or countries together for the inspection.
4. Public officials cooperate together for establishing the policy.
5. Public officials cooperate together for both establishing and implementing the policy.

The result shows that there is a not so strong relationship among neighbors in most municipalities, and only a few cities cooperate together for establishing or implementing the policy.

Concerning the question of the Vertical Determinant Model, the answers are classified into five groups on the basis of the strength of relationship between the central government and prefectures. As the number is bigger, the vertical relation becomes stronger, and in municipalities with a strong relation, the central government and prefectures give great influence not only on the establishment of the policy, but also to its implementation in municipalities. The result is shown in **Figure 4-3**.

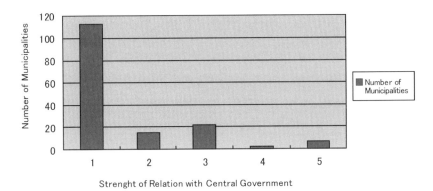

Figure 4-3 The result of the Vertical Determinant Mode

Q3. Question on the Vertical Determinant Model

How strong is the relationship between the central government and prefectures in the establishment and implementation of the social welfare policy for elderly?

(Choose one from five choices)

1. There is almost no relationship between the central government and prefectures or is only the regular meeting in order to exchange information.
2. Public officials cooperate with the center for studying and researching the policy.
3. Public officials in both local and central governments visit proceeding cities or countries together for the inspection.
4. Public officials cooperate with the center for establishing the policy.
5. Public officials cooperate with the center for both establishing and implementing the policy.

The results show that there is a not so strong personal relationship with the central government in most municipalities,

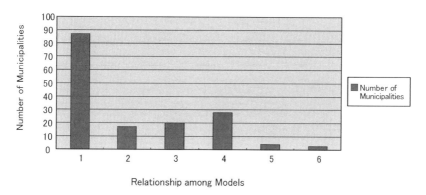

Figure 4-4 The result of the relation among models

and only a few cities cooperate together for establishing or implementing the policy.

Concerning the question of the relationship among the three models, the answers are classified into five groups. Public officials choose 1 in the case where the Internal Determinant Model can be considered as the most suitable model, and choose 5 in the case where the Vertical Determinant Model can be considered as most applicable for the status quo. As the number is getting smaller, public officials make much of the needs of the residents for the policy and environment of municipalities, and as the number is getting larger, the public officials tend more to establish the policy by following the standards and guidelines of the center. The result is shown in **Figure 4-4**.

Q4. Question on the relation among three models

Which actors are considered most influential to the policy process?

(Choose 1 one form six patterns of the relation)

1. Factors causing local governments to establish the policy are political, economic, and social characteristics of municipalities.
2. Neighboring municipalities play the most important role for local governments to establish the policy.
3. Both characteristics of municipalities and relation among neighbors are most important among the three actors.
4. Three actors, characteristics of municipalities, relation among neighbors, and the influence of the center are all very important at the same level.
5. Both relationships among neighbors and with the central government are most important among the three actors.
6. The relation between the central government and prefectures is the most influential among the three actors.

According to the results of the research, public officials in about 70% of all municipalities answered to decide their polities by the factors classified into the Internal Determinant Model. In other words, in the minds of public officials, factors classified into both the Regional Diffusion Model and the Vertical Determinant Model do not influence so greatly, and most public officials think for themselves in order to decide their policy by their own will.

By using the results of this research, I would like to consider the following two points: the relationship among models, and which Vertical Determinant Model between the two will be more suitable for implementing Japanese policy process.

Concerning the relationship among models, the Internal Determinant Model is the most applicable among the three, and the other two models are not suitable so much for the status quo in the consciousness of public officials. In about 70% of municipalities, public officials attach importance mostly to the needs of residents for the policy, and they do not consider so much the relationship among neighboring municipalities, nor with the central government. Therefore, concerning the second question, which types of the Vertical Determinant Model will be more suitable, the answer can be considered as the Compulsory Vertical Determinant Model, because public officials do not follow the center by their intention.

As I described above, the Compulsory Vertical Determinant Model is more applicable for Japanese policy process than the Voluntary Vertical Determinant Model, because public officials do not intend to follow the policy of the center, but they actively try to consider the needs of residents as being the most important factor. However, finally, the social welfare policy is decided and implemented by the Vertical Determinant Model, and there will be the overall system of bureaucracy which greatly influences public officials in local governments to compulsory follow the center.

The next important question will be the relationship between the three models and the outcome of the policies. In other words, which types of policy process can bring about the most satisfactory policy for the residents? "Most satisfactory" means the policy which fits the needs for the policy for the residents in the best way, or in other words, the level of satisfaction for the policy from residents which is highest from among the policies. Because the policy which can most satisfy residents within budgetary constrictions can be considered as the best policy, we should consider the most ideal policy

90   Chapter 4

process as that which can bring about the best policy for the residents. By using the results of the research interviews on the three models, I will try to answer the question in the next section.

2. RELATION BETWEEN MODELS AND POLICY PERFORMANCE

From the discussion before this session, we can understand that the social welfare policy for the elderly in Japan has been established and implemented via the policy process which is described as the Vertical Determinant Model in this book. Not only the era of the Gold Plan, but also under the period of current decentralization reforms, the basic policy process has not changed so greatly. This point is clarified by the results of the analysis on Hypothesis I, where the Vertical Determinant Model is most applicable for the social welfare policy compared to other policy areas.

As many authors have mentioned in preceding research, and as I have also described in the former part of this book, there exists the great limitation on the Vertical Determinant Model, or the policy process that the central government establishes the main policy and local governments implement it faithfully. Because the social welfare policy is the policy area that should be established to fit the daily needs of residents, and the needs of residents are completely different depending on the area, the basic policy which is established by the central government cannot fit the variety of needs of local residents. Even though the central government changed

Quality of Policy and Three Models 91

the priority of social welfare policy for the elderly from welfare facilities to the in-home services, at present residents are not willing to use the in-home services even after the Long-Term Insurance System established in 2000[1]. We can know from these examples that the Vertical Determinant Model itself is no longer deemed respectable for Japanese society.

Seen broadly, the social welfare policy for the elderly in Japan is established and implemented by the Vertical Determinant Model. However, upon considering the details, there are some exceptions in this theory, and in some proceeding municipalities, public officials determine their policy via different processes, and also, some policies in social welfare are proceeded by a different model.

There are a lot of policies and programs in social welfare policy for the elderly, and some of them garner great satisfaction from the residents. The programs that have high satisfaction from the residents are the day services among programs in the insurance system, and precautions and other special programs for the wealthier members of the elderly among programs out with the insurance system. Satisfaction levels from the residents of these services are very high throughout

---

[1] This tendency of usage was found in several interviews with the public officials who had taken charge of social welfare policy for elderly in small cities and villages. In these areas, residents are always nervous about how they appear to the neighborhoods, and there is the common sense among them that using these services is not respectable. Therefore, compared to getting the welfare facilities, residents tend to hesitate to use in-home services. Also, they do not feel like having strangers come to their house even if they are home helpers who are admitted by the public officials.

Japan according to several research papers[2]. As the results of the analysis for Hypothesis II, these services are brought about by the policy process of the Internal Determinant Model, and concerning the relationship between the models and policy performance, the most desirable policy process, or the ideal model can be understood as the Internal Determinant Model. Therefore, if we can establish the system that other kinds of services, which are mainly brought about by the Vertical Determinant Model currently, are established via the policy process of the Internal Determinant Model, public officials in local governments will be able to establish and implement more satisfactory policies to the residents.

In order to change the existing policy process, from the Vertical to the Internal, what kind of policies will be needed? I will consider this point next by using the research interviews in three proceeding municipalities in the area of social welfare policy. The municipalities, which I pick up here, are Musashino City and Mitaka City in Tokyo, and Takanosu Town in Akita Prefecture. Both Musashino City and Mitaka City are very urbanized cities in Tokyo and have succeeded in supplying very satisfactory policies to the residents. However, even though both of the cities have the Internal Determinant

---

[2] As I described in the former part of the book, in social welfare policy for elderly, public officials attach great importance to the day services and precautions based on the needs from the residents in almost 121 cities according to the research for public officials in municipalities. Also, in the research interviews with the public officials in Musashino City, Mitaka City, and Takanosu Town, which are typical of proceeding municipalities in social welfare policy areas in Japan, we can know that public officials in these cities also put priority on the day services and precautions because satisfaction levels of the policy from the residents is highest with regards to these services.

Quality of Policy and Three Models   93

policy processes, the mechanism of the policy process itself is completely different between two cities.

On the other hand, Takanosu Town is not an urbanized city, rather, it is a small village with a high percentage of the elderly within the population. It is not a wealthy municipality, but residents in the village greatly satisfied with the social welfare policy in the city. This village also has the Internal Determinant policy process, but the detail of the process is completely different from the two urbanized cities[3].

There was a long trial period to develop the social welfare policy in Musashino City, which is a very urbanized municipality in Tokyo, and it established its social welfare policy earlier than the central government. The long history of the trial was made possible by the wealthy budget of the city. Because Musashino City is the place where rich people tend to gather to live, the level of revenue has been much higher than in other municipalities. This is the fundamental reason for the city being able to establish the proceeding welfare policies in the Internal Determinant policy process earlier than other municipalities. Among variables in the Internal Determinant Model, those of the social and economic environment, such as the percentage of the elderly living with their children, the percentage of house possession, the total expenditure for the social welfare policy, and the growth of revenue, are greatly influential upon the policy process of the city. Also, residents in the city have been very conscious of the social welfare policy from the early period of its implementation, and that is why public officials began to focus on the policy earlier than

[3] The research interviews with these three municipalities were carried out in February, 2004.

the central government. The policy has been established under the strong leadership of public officials in this city, not the bureaucrats in the central government, and this can be considered as an exemplary policy process for public officials in other local governments to follow.

In Mitaka City, which is also a very urbanized city in Tokyo and closely located to Musashino City, the Internal Determinant policy process was established by the cooperation between public officials and residents. Even though both cities have similar characteristics of an urbanized city, the budget conditions are different. Because of the budgetary limit of the city, public officials in Mitaka City had to consider different ways of establishing the Internal Determinant policy process. They tried to establish proceeding policy via cooperation with residents so that they could supply satisfactory services under the budget constraints. "Strong cooperation between public officials and residents" is the main factor for this city being able to establish its very satisfactory policy for its residents. The citizens of the city have also been very conscious of the social welfare policy from its early period, and they have tried to participate with the policy process very positively. Even though the policy in this city has been established by the strong leadership of public officials, as with Musashino City, which is the typical example of the Internal Determinant policy process, positive participation of the residents with the policy process has also enabled public officials to supply very satisfactory programs.

In Takanosu Town, on the other hand, the strong leadership of the mayor has been the main factor in establishing the proceeding social welfare policy for the elderly. Because

Quality of Policy and Three Models   95

Takanosu Town is very rural region where the percentage of the elderly among residents is high, and the budget is not in a good condition, the mayor had a sense of the impending crisis concerning the future of the village. He began to establish the plan to make Takanosu Town as the best place for the elderly to live in, and visited Denmark to gather a lot of information on the social welfare policy. By getting strong support from the public officials and residents, the mayor pushed forward with the proceeding policies. The quality of the services, which are supplied in Takanosu Town, is much higher than the national minimum standard level, and the positive attitude of mayor toward social welfare policy is the main factor that enables the village to establish such a highly satisfactory policy process.

These three examples demonstrate the fact that there are many kinds of actors who create great impact upon the satisfactory implementation of policy process even though they are all classified into the Internal Determinant Model. Among these variables, the strong leadership of the mayor in Takanosu Town and the wealthy budgetary conditions in Musashino City are both not so common relative to other municipalities because both factors are greatly related to the peculiarity of mayor and residents. However, establishing the cooperative relationship between public officials and residents in Mitaka City can be common example to other municipalities in order to establish the Internal Determinant policy process. Even though most municipalities do not have good conditions for the implementation of social welfare policy, namely that they do not have enough budget resources, nor have the strong mayor required, public officials will be able to establish the satisfactory social welfare policy by cooperating with residents, even under such budget constraints. In other words, all municipalities have the possibility to cope with their idiosyncratic difficulties and can establish a satisfactory social welfare policy for elderly by contriving to establish their own policy process in conjunction with residents.

If so, what kind of system or policy will be needed to establish the Internal Determinant policy process in most municipalities without the chaotic situation where public officials are getting used to the Vertical Determinant policy process?

3. CONSIDERATION OF THE RESULTS

Concerning the relationship between the policy process (or applicable model) and the policy performance (or level of satisfaction of residents toward the policy), we can know the following three points from the results of several research papers and analysis.

Firstly, as I have described before, public officials in municipalities try to put priority to the needs of residents vis-à-vis the policy and try to establish the policy which can best satisfy residents as much as possible in their minds. In other words, most public officials support the system change from the Vertical to the Internal. However, in practice, most public officials implement their policy by following the center, and there is already the complete Vertical Determinant policy processes in place and which are deeply related to the national grants, strict rules, regulations, and other hidden dimensions of the pre-existing bureaucracy.

Quality of Policy and Three Models 97

Concerning the relationship between the policy process and its performance, the Internal Determinant Model is most desirable as I have mentioned before. This is because policies that are implemented by the Internal Determinant policy process are very satisfactory to the residents throughout Japan. Also, in some proceeding municipalities, public officials commonly establish their policies through the Internal Determinant policy process. However, in actual policy process in most municipalities in Japan, the social welfare policy for the elderly has been established and implemented through the Vertical Determinant policy process, and moreover, it is not the Voluntary one in which public officials follow the policy of the center by *their* intention, but the Compulsory one in which public officials have to follow the policy because of *the system*, such as national grants and regulations. Therefore, in order to change the policy process itself, we should push forward with the current decentralization reforms with the transformation of at least two systems. One is the change of laws and regulations, and the other is the downsizing of several national grants.

Firstly, in order to let local governments establish their own policies more freely, several kinds of laws and regulations should be abolished. Under the current centralized system, public officials in municipalities have to get admission or permission from central governments and prefectures to do something new, and this system can be considered as the root of the Vertical Determinant policy process. Now, in some of the proceeding municipalities, public officials and residents cooperate to establish the new social welfare policy, which is called the "Community Welfare Plan," and this process can be understood as the beginning of establishing the Internal

Determinant policy process in all municipalities[4]. By changing the system and getting rid of current, too strict rules and regulations, local government will be able to establish their own policy more freely.

Secondly, in order to change the current centralized system, national grants should be abolished gradually. By supplying grants to peculiar programs, the central government permits local ones to follow their own will because most local governments tend to pick up the programs in order to get national grants. This system is harmful for local governments because, not only can they not establish their own policies, but furthermore, they will become lazy in gathering their own budget from their residents. These two basic systematic changes will be necessary, of course, and the current decentralization process of Japanese society should be propelled more strongly by including these systematic changes.

However, the problem is that the decentralization reform process itself has been established by the central government, not be propelled by the positive participation of prefectures and municipalities. Therefore, in the current mindset of Japanese society, where the compulsory decentralization reform is proceeding at really high speed, many municipalities are not

---

[4] The "Community Welfare Plan" began to become established after the basic laws of social welfare policy were completely changed in June, 2000. By changing the centralized policy process, the central government did not establish the main plan, and each municipality can make their own by cooperating with residents. Because most public officials are not used to establishing their own plans, and because they have only the experience of following the policy of the center and implementing it faithfully, many local governments have difficulty establishing the Community Welfare Plan. They are struggling very hard now, but in some proceeding municipalities, the new plans are beginning to be established in cooperation among several actors.

Quality of Policy and Three Models 99

adequately prepared to cope with the dramatic system change. Concerning the social welfare policy, many small municipalities cannot supply welfare services even at the national minimum standard level. Although the basic policy of social welfare in Japan is to guarantee that all Japanese citizens are able to get at least the minimum social welfare services without reference to their jobs and living areas, and the dramatic decentralization damages the basic policy itself. Therefore, we should establish the policy that can change the system more gradually so that the local governments, which are getting used to the Vertical Determinant policy process, can change themselves in order to establish the Internal Determinant policy process.

The several analyses in this book will offer propitious suggestions toward establishing the new policy for a more gradual decentralization. In this book, I would also like to especially focus on the Regional Diffusion Model whose characteristic is in the midpoint between the Internal Determinant Model and the Vertical Determinant Model. By establishing the Regional Diffusion policy process, which will enable even small municipalities to fit their policy processes to their own Internal Determinant Model, there will be the possibility that the systematic change of policy processes, from the Vertical Determinant Model to the Internal Determinant Model, will be more smoothly propelled by public officials in local governments themselves without any ensuing chaos. In the final chapter, I will focus on new possibility of the Regional Diffusion policy process and try to clarify the whole image of Japanese bureaucracy.

CHAPTER 5
DECENTRALIZATION AND POLICY PROCESS

1. SCALE OF MUNICIPALITIES AND HYPOTHESIS

In the former chapter, I did not distinguish the difference between municipalities in terms of scale. Even though there is not so much difference between municipalities in Japan as compared to those in the United States, where a decentralized system has completely penetrated throughout the country, municipalities in Japan also have a variety of sizes and populations. Therefore, the characteristics, the needs of the residents vis-à-vis policy, and the mechanism of policy process implementation of these municipalities are all very different depending on their scale.

The analyses in former chapters did not distinguish between the differences of municipalities, but distinguishing those in relation to the characteristics among policies and programs was the main focus. However, as I described in former chapters, municipalities can be classified into several models depending on their characteristics, and in order to consider the concrete policy process for establishing a decentralized Japanese society, we have to classify the difference between municipalities in order to effectively consider the different needs of different policy processes.

Decentralization and Policy Process 101

There have been several articles that discuss the relationship between the characteristics of municipalities and mechanisms of policy process, and many have mentioned that the mechanism of policy process, the strength of influence from the center, and relationship among neighboring municipalities are all different depending on the difference of scale of municipalities. For example, Soga[1] mentioned that there is a trade-off relationship between the level of constraint of movement among areas and the strength of influence from the central government. The influence of the center is much greater in villages where the level of constrain of movement among areas is higher than the cities where people can move freely among various areas. One hypothesis emerging from the results of the analysis of Soga is that the Internal Determinant Model is more applicable for city scenarios, and the Vertical Determinant Model is more applicable to villages.

Of course, there are some villages, like Takanosu Village that can introduce the proceeding polices in the Internal Determinant policy process, and in some large cities, public officials establish the policy in the Vertical Determinant policy process. However, in this chapter, I would like to make the discussion easier for statistical analyses because these exceptions are very few in a centralized society. The new hypothesis is described in **Figure 5-1,** which shows the relationship among the scale of municipalities, abundance of budget, strength of leadership of particular municipality in the special welfare district, and number of municipalities for which hypothesis are applicable.

---

[1] Soga K., *op. cit.*

Chapter 5

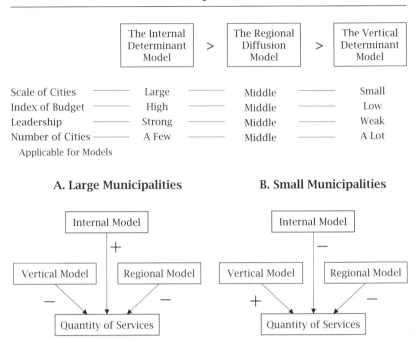

Figure 5-1 Regulating Factors of Policy Process and Scale of Municipalities

Here, I would like to analyze the relationship between the scale of municipalities and the three models in order to figure out what kind of policies are necessary for Japanese municipalities to establish the Internal Determinant policy process. The hypotheses for analysis are as follows.

Hypothesis III-1:
The Internal Determinant Model is more applicable for large cities while the Vertical Determinant Model is more suitable for small municipalities.

Hypothesis III-2:
The Regional Diffusion Model is most applicable for the middle scale municipalities.

Decentralization and Policy Process   103

The results of the Multiple Regression Analysis on hypothesis III-1 and III-2 are shown in **Figure 5-2** where independent variables are the "frequency of use of the home-visit service per 100 elderly who need care" and the "number of beds in special nursing homes per 100 elderly who need care," and several variables describing three models are dependent variables. Most variables are the same in the former analysis, but in this case, variables are classified into three groups according to the scale of the municipalities in question.

Firstly, I would like to consider the results of the analysis for hypothesis III-1. Concerning the home-visit service, variables in the Internal Determinant Model are most applicable to large municipalities and variables in the Vertical Determinant Model are not influential at all. In more detail, among variables in the Internal Determinant Model, the quantity of services is decided by the needs of the residents for the In-home services, such as the percentage of elderly in a specific population, and that of the elderly who need care among all elderly persons overall. As the scale of municipalities becomes smaller, variables in the Vertical Determinant Model become more applicable in addition to the variables in the Internal Determinant Model. Same kinds of variables in the Internal Determinant Model, such as the percentage of elderly in population, and that of elderly who need care from among all elderly are also influential upon small municipalities, but in addition, the strength of relationship with the central government and prefectures become more influential to the policy process as the scale of municipalities becomes smaller. Additionally, in small villages and towns, the progressiveness of the mayor to the social welfare policy (in the Internal Determinant Model) and national aid and budgetary relationship with the

	Quantity of Home-visit services			Quantity of Welfare Facilities		
	Large Municipalities	Middle Municipalities	Small Municipalities	Large Municipalities	Middle Municipalities	Small Municipalities
Internal Model						
Increase of elderly	-.134**	-.303+		-.672**	-.589***	-.256**
Elderly need care	-.218***	-.217**	-.252**	-.736**	-.343***	-.334***
Service Industry		-.380**		-.075*	-.221*	.167*
Expenditure	.082*		.213**		.460**	.540***
Growth of Revenue			.108*		.163**	
Gap of Population					-.167*	
Elderly with child			-.135*		-.268***	
House Possession						.163*
Attitude for welfare			.126*			.128*
Regional Model						
Population Gap	-.285***	-.247*	-.356***		.183*	
Number of cities		.158*	-.172*		.241*	
Population in area						
Quantity of Services	.433***	.200**	.617***		.232***	
Vertical Model						
Index of Finance		.251*				
Past Record B		.251*				
Past Record C		.226*				
Accomplish Rate						
Central Grant			.104**	.119**	.145*	
Prefecture Grant						
Regular Allocation						-.253***
Special Allocation			.301*			-.241**
R-square	.140	.453	.326	.210	.257	.326
Number	715	715	715	715	715	715

0 ≤ *** < 0.005   0.005 ≤ ** < 0.01   0.01 ≤ * < 0.05   0.05 ≤ + < 0.1

Figure 5-2 Results of Analysis on Hypothesis III

Decentralization and Policy Process 105

center (in the Vertical Determinant Model) also become very influential variables. In other words, public officials in large municipalities can decide on the quantity of service relative to the needs of residents for the policy, but in the middle level municipalities, officials also have to consider the relationship between the center and prefectures. In small municipalities, the progressiveness of mayors toward social welfare policy and budgetary relationships is also very influential, and public officials cannot establish the policy by their own will alone. Therefore, hypothesis III-1 can be understood as supportable.

On the contrary, concerning the welfare facilities for the elderly, the overall budgetary condition is most influential to all scales of municipalities. In addition, in middle scale municipalities, variables in the Regional Diffusion Model and in the Vertical Determinant Model are also influential upon the policy process. In small scale municipalities, budgetary relationships with the central government have great impact upon the quantity of service rather than political factors. Moreover, in these municipalities, among variables pertaining to the Internal Determinant Model, the environment of the community and political factors are also very influential compared in comparison with the middle or large-scale municipalities. The Internal Determinant Model is applicable for all scales you must of municipalities, but the Vertical Determinant Model is applicable only for small municipalities. Therefore, concerning the welfare facilities for the elderly , hypothesis III-1 cannot be considered as strongly supportable.

Next, concerning the hypothesis III-2, it can be considered as supportable only for In-home services, as we can get the same result via hypothesis III-1. Concerning the In-home services, hypothesis III-2 is very supportable, but concerning the welfare facilities, the result is completely different, and the Regional Diffusion Model is applicable only in middle scale municipalities. The relationship among neighboring municipalities creates great impact on policy process only in the middle scale municipalities, and in large and small municipalities, it is not so important. The reason for this result can be understood in that elderly can join the nursing home in different municipalities, but they cannot use home-help services in neighboring municipalities. Therefore, concerning the hypothesis III-2, it can be understood as supportable only for the In-home services.

From these results, we can know that the applicable models or the mechanisms of policy process are different depending on the scale of the municipalities in question. In other words, the Internal Determinant Model is most applicable for lager municipalities, the Regional Diffusion Model is most suitable for middle scale cities, and the Vertical Determinant Model is most applicable for small municipalities.

Presently in Japan, the central government is trying hard to decentralize the policy process mechanisms throughout Japanese society. This reform is current very rapidly, and it is apparent that the influence of the Vertical Determinant policy process is becoming much weaker, and the Internal Determinant policy process will become the main policy process even in small municipalities. From the results of several research projects undertaken and analyses given in this book, we have already known that the most ideal policy process is the Internal Determinant one, and the principle of the decentralization reform itself can be considered as correct.

However, because this reform is also a very centralized policy, and also transpiring very rapidly, small municipalities cannot keep up with this pace of reform. Public officials who are getting used to the Vertical Determinant policy process cannot transfer so rapidly to the Internal one. Therefore, in these municipalities, residents cannot get services even at the minimum standard level, and this is certainly not desirable considering the nature of social welfare.

In order to establish the Internal Determinant policy process in these small municipalities, it is apparent that additional policy or system mechanisms will be needed, and I would like to focus on the Regional Diffusion Model, which has both merits and demerits and whose characteristics are situated at the midpoint between the Internal and the Vertical models. The Regional Diffusion policy process can be considered ideal in cases where the proceeding municipality greatly influences its neighbors toward establishing the same level of services. On the contrary, it can also be harmful that there are no proceeding municipalities around and where neighboring municipalities are not willing to establish the proceeding policy. Therefore, by establishing the systems that the Regional Diffusion Model can make a positive influence, and save the small municipalities, the Internal Determinant policy process can be established more smoothly and easily.

2. SAFETY NET AND POLICY PROCESS

As noted above, in order to establish the Internal Determinant policy process more smoothly and without chaos, we have to establish the additional policy that enables municipalities to

108   Chapter 5

change from the Vertical Determinant policy process to the
Internal one more easily, and the main focus of the policy is
to establish the system of the Regional Diffusion policy process
in order to save small municipalities.

As has been mentioned in several articles and materials,
there is the group-oriented culture called "Groupism" in Japanese[2] and this culture has penetrated deep within the consciousness of Japanese. Therefore, urgent decentralization
cannot fit comfortably within a group-oriented society like
Japan, but rather, more gradual decentralization will be suitable. By establishing the policy process that leading municipalities can take the leadership role to implement the ideal policy,
and neighbors can cooperate together toward imitation of this,
all municipalities in a particular area will be able to have much
the same level of social welfare policy.

Figure 5-3 describes the image of establishing the Regional
Diffusion policy process. In case A, there is one proceeding
municipality in the area, but there is no cooperation with
neighbors. This is the case of Municipality A in Chapter 2. In
the Regional Diffusion Policy Process, because the leading
municipality has the power and responsibility to establish the
same level of social welfare policy in neighboring municipalities, the leader and follower have to cooperate with each other.

There are some areas which have already established the
Regional Diffusion Policy Process in Japan as with case B.
This is the case of Municipality B in Chapter 2. In this case,
there have been historical and/or cultural relationships among
residents, and public officials have also been very cooperative

---

[2] Jun, J.S., "The Hidden Dimension of Japanese Administration: Culture
and Its Impact", *Public Administration Review*, vol.55, pp.125-134.

Case A: The leading municipality should cooperate with neighbors

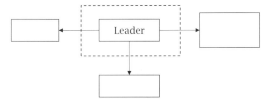

Case B: Ideal Regional Diffusion Policy Process

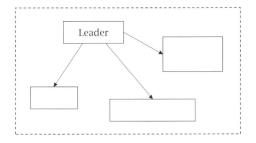

Case C: Neighboring municipality should be merged in order to improve the ability of policy formation and implementation

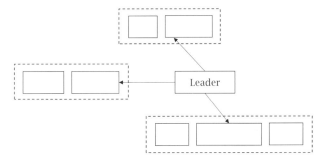

Figure 5-3 Regional Diffusion Policy Process

with neighbors in establishing and implementing the social welfare policy. This can be understood as the *ideal* case, and similar systems should be established even in areas where there is no cooperative relationship among neighbors historically and/or culturally.

In case C, the neighboring municipalities are too small to catch up with the policy of the leading municipality. This is the case of Municipality C in Chapter 2. In this case, neighboring municipalities have to merge with each other to attain a certain level of pre-requisite ability to be able to establish and implement the new policy in the first instance. Subsequently, the leading municipality should take its leadership role for improving the policy of neighbors. There are a lot of small towns and villages as in case C in Japan, and many municipalities are now trying hard to merge with each other.

We can imagine the possibility that some leading municipalities are not willing to take leadership roles toward their neighbors because the Regional Diffusion policy process can become buttons on while they are attempting to improve their own policy while also implementing it. However, considering the nature of social welfare policy, these leading municipalities have to cooperate with neighbors regardless because everyone can imagine the danger that leading municipalities become followers by way of unexpected disasters. Social welfare is the policy whose character is relatively cooperative, and even leading municipalities cannot know the future. Such Regional Diffusion policy process can be considered as ideal to all municipalities in a group-oriented society like Japan, and this will be the next system of Japanese Bureaucracy.

3. IMAGES OF JAPANESE BUREAUCRACY

Japanese Bureaucracy has traditionally been very strong. It is not because Japan is a centralized society, but because the social system itself was, and continues to be, established by public officials. As has been described in this book, Japanese Bureaucracy is now changing dramatically and will keep transforming in the future, but the fundamental system in which the mechanisms of society are basically formed by bureaucrats will not be changed easily. It is the Japanese way. The three main policy processes- the Internal Determinant policy process, the Regional Diffusion policy process, and the Vertical Determinant policy process- are all related to public administrators, although each of them has a different relationship with the central government and among neighboring municipalities. This is the public system of Japanese society which is brought about and is kept in a constant state of change by the power of Japanese Bureaucracy.

REFERENCES

Abbey, A. and Andrews, F.M., "Modeling the Psychological Determinants of Life Quality", *Social Indicators Research*, vol.16, 1985, pp.1-34.

Aberbach, J. et al., *Bureaucratis and Politicians in Western Democracy*, Harvard Univ. Press, 1981.

ACIR, *The Role of Equalization in Federal Grants*, January 1964.

Adamns, C. F., Landsbergen, D. Jr., and Cobler, L., "Welfare Reform and Paternity, Establishment: A Social Experiment", *Journal of Policy Analysis and Management*, vol. 11, no.4, 1992, pp.665-687.

Adams, G.B. and Balfour, D.L, *Unmasking Administrative Evil*, SAGA Publications, 1998, pp. 107-180.

Alborw, M., *Bureaucracy*, Pall Mall Press, 1970.

Alderfer, H.F., *Local Government in Developing Countries*, McGraw-Hill, 1964.

Alexander, E. R., "Improbable Implementation: The Pressman-Wildavsky Paradox Revisited", *Journal of Public Policy*, vol.9, 1989, pp. 451-465.

Alteriis, M. D., "Local Governmetns as Implementators of Public Policy", *Policy Studies Review*, vol.9, no.4, 1990, pp.756-773.

Alvarez, R.M., Nagler, J., and Bowler, S., "Issues, Economics, and the Dynamics of Multiparty Elections: The British 1987 General Election", *American Political Science Review*, vol.94, no.1, 2000, pp. 131-146.

Amakawa, A., *Regionalism and Autonomy: The Continuing Debate in Japan, A Paper prepared for the Conference on Local Institutions in National Development: Strategies and Consequence of Local national Linkage in the Industrial Democracies*, Bellagio, Italy, March 15-19, 1982.

Anderson, J. E., *Public Policy-Making*, Praeger Publishers, Inc., 1975.

Anderson, R., "Equality and Equal Opportunity for Welfare", *Philosophical Studies*, vol.56, 1989, pp.77-93.

Anderson, G. M., Shughart II W. F., and Tollison, R. D., "A public choice theory of the great contraciton", *Public Choice*, vol.59, 1988, pp.3-23.

Anheier, H. K., "An Elabolate Network: Profiling the Third sector in Germany", in Gidron B., Kramer, R.M., and Salamon, L. M. eds., *Government and The Third Sector: Emerging Relationshipis in Welfare States*, Jossey –Bass, 1992.

Apter, D., *Choice and Politics of Allocation*, Yale Univ. Press, 1971.

Arent, H., *The Origins of Totaliarism*, Harcourt, 1951.

Arrow, K. J., *The Limits of Organization*, Norton, 1974.

Arrow, K. J., *Social Choice and Individual Values*, New York: Wiley, 1951, 2nd.ed., 1963.

References 113

Ashford, D. E., "The Structural Comparison of Social Policy and International Politics", *Policy and Politics*, vol.12, no.4, 1984.

Ashford, D. E., *British Dogmatism and French Pragmatism: Central-Local Relations in the Welfare State*, London and Boston: Allen and Unwin, 1982.

Ashford, D. E., *National Resrouces and Urban Polichy*, Methuen, 1990.

Ashford, D. E., "Decentralizing Welfare States: Social Policies and Intergovernmental Policies", Dente, B. and Kjellberg, F. eds., *The Dynamics of Institutiolan Change: Local Government Reorganization in Western Democracies*, London: Saga, 1998.

R. Axelrod, *The Evolution of Cooperation*, Basic Books.

Baldock, J., "Culture: The Missing Variables in Understanding Social Policy?", *Social Policy and Administration*, vol.33, no.4, 1999, pp.458-473.

Bane, J. M. and Ellwood, D., *Welfare Realities: From Rhetric to Reform*, Harvard University Press, 1998.

Barker, F., *Organizational Systems*, Homewood, 1973.

Barret, D., "Older peoples' experiences of Community Care", *Social Policy and Aministration*, vol.26, no.4, 1992, pp.296-312.

Barry, N., *Welfare*, Open University Press, 1999.

Baumol, W.J., "Macroeconomics of Unbalanced Growth: The Anatomy of Urban Crisis", *American Economic Review*, vol.57, 1967.

Bayley, L.B., *Local Government-It Is Manageble*, Pergamon Press, 1979.

Beer, S., "Federalism, Nationalism and Democracy in America", *American Political Science Review*, vol.72, 1978.

Bendor, J., Taylor, S., and Galen, R.V., "Stacking the Deck: Bureaucratic Missions and Policy Design", *American Political Science Review*, vol.87, no.3, 1987, pp.873-896.

Bergson, A., "A Reformulation of Certain Aspects of Welfare Economics", *Quarterly Journal of Economics*, vol.52, 1938, pp.310-334.

Berman, P., "The Study of Macro-Implementation and Micro-Implementation", *Public Policy*, Vol.26, No2, 1978.

Berry, M. E., "Confrontation at the National Conference on Social Welfare", *Social Service Review*, vol.60, no.3, 1986, pp. 360-377.

Berry, W. D., Berkman, M.B., and Schneiderman, S., "Legislative Professionalism and Incumbent Reelection: The Development of Institutional Boundaries", *American Political Science Review*, vol.94, no.4, 2000, pp.859-872.

Billis, D., *Welfare Bureaucracy: Their Design and Change in Response to Social Problems*, Heinemann Educational Books Ltd., 1984.

Billis, D. and Clennerster, H., "Human Services and the Voluntary Sector: Towards a Theory of Comparative Advantage", *Journal of Social Policy*, vol.27, no.1, pp.79-98.

Birkland, T. A., *An Introduction to the Policy Process: Theories, Concepts, and Models of Public Policy Making*, M.E. Shape, 2001.

Blackman, T., "Facing Up to Underfunding: Equity and Resrenchment in Community Care", *Social Policy and Administration*, vol.32, no.2, 1998, pp.182-195.

Blau, J., "Theories of the Welfare State", *Social Science Review*, vol.63, no.1, 1989, pp.26-38.

Bonoli, G., "Classifying Welfare State: a Two-dimension Approach", *Journal of Social Policy*, vol.26, no.3, 1997, pp.351-372.

Booth, T., Bilson, A., and Fowell, I., "Staff Attitudes and Caring Practices in Homes for the Elderly", *British Journal of Social Work*, vol.20, 1990, pp.117-131.

Bolman, L.G. and Deal, T.E., *Reframing Organizations*, Jossey-Bass Publishers, 1997.

Bollens, J. C. and Schmandt, H.T., *The Metropolis, Its People, politics, and Economic life*, Second Edition, New York: Harper & Row, Publishers, 1970.

Boreham, P., Hall, R. and Leet, M., "Labour and Citizenship: The Development of Welfare State Regimes", *Journal of Public Policy*, vol.16, no.2, 1996, pp.203-227.

Borge, L., "Economic and political determinatns of fee income in Norwegian local governmetns", *Public Choices*, vol.83, 1995, pp.353-375.

Bortheman, P., Hall, R. and Leet, M., "Labour and Citizenship: The Development of Welfare State Regimes", *Journal of Pubic Policy*, vol.16, no.2, 1996, pp.203-227.

Bouchaert, G, "Efficiency measurement from a management perspective: a case of the Civil Registry Office in Flanders", *International Review of Administrative Sciences*, vol.59, 1993, pp.11-27.

Boushel, M.," What Kind of People are We? 'Race', Anti-Racism and Social Welfare Research", *British Journal of Social Work*, vol.30, 2000, pp.449-463.

Bovaird, T. and Mallinson, I., "Setting Objectives and Measuring Achievement in Social Care", *British Journal of Social Work*, vol.18, 1988, pp.309-324.

Bovens, M., *The Quest for Responsibility*, Cambridge University Press, 1998.

Box, T.C., *Citizen Governance*, SAGA Publications, 1998.

Bradshaw, Y., Kendall, I., Blackmore, M., Johnson, N. and Jenkinson, S., "Complaining Our Way to Quality: Complaints, Contracts and the Voluntary Sector", *Social Policy and Administration*, vol.32, no.3, 1998, pp.209-225.

Braybrook, D., and Lindblim, C. E., *A Strategy of Decision*, Free Press, 1963.

Brehem, J. and Rahn, W., "Individual-Level Evidence for the Causes and Consequences of SocialCapital", *American Journal of Political Sicence*, vol.41, no.3, 1997, pp.999-1023.

References 115

Brenton, M., *The Voluntary Sector in British Services*, Longman, 1985.

Brinton, M. C., "Social capital in the Japanese youth labor market: Labor market policy, schools, and norms", *Policy Sciences*, vol.33, 2000, pp.289-306.

Broadbent, J. P., "Social capital and labor politics in Japan: Cooperation or cooptation?", *Policy Sciences*, vol.33, 2000, pp.307-321.

Brodkin, E. Z., "Inside the Welfare Contract: Discretion and Accountability in State Welfare Administration", *Social Service Review*, vol.71, no.1, 1997, pp.1-33.

Brown, R.D., "Party Cleavages and Welfare Effort in the American States", *American Political Science Review*, vol.89, no.1, 1995, pp.23-33.

Brown, D.S. and Hunter, W., "Democracy and Social Spending in Latin America, 1980-92", *American Political Science Review*, vol.93, 1999, pp.779-790.

Bruno Dente and Francesco Kjellberg (eds.), *The Dynamics of Institutional Change: Local Government Reorganization in Western Democracies*, Saga Publications, 1988

Bulmer, M., Lewis, J., and Piachaud, D., *The Goals of Social Policy*, Unwin Hyman Ltd., 1989.

Butter, F. A. and Morgan, M. S. eds., *Empirical Models and Policy-Making: Interaction and Institutions*, Routledge, 2000.

Caiden, G. E., *Administration Reform*, Aldin Publishing Co., 1969.

Calder, K.E., "Elites in an Equalizing Role: Ex-Bureaucrats as Coordinators and Intermedeiariteis in the Japanese Government-Business Relationship", *Comparative Politics*, vol.21, 1989, pp.379-404.

Carley, M., *Rational Techniques in Policy Analysis*, Heinemann Educational Books, 1980.

Carmichael, P., "Analysing Political Choice in Local Government: A Compartive Case Study Approack", *Public Administration*, vol.72, 1994, pp.241-262.

Casetti E. and Jones, J. P., "Spatial Parameter Variation by Orthogonal Trend Surface Expansion: An Application to the Analysisi of Welfare Program Participation Rates", *Social Service Review*, vol.63, no.4, 1989, pp.630-656.

Clark P. B. and Wilson, J. Q., "Incentive System: A Theory of Organizations", *Administratie Science Quarterly*, vol.6, 1961.

Clark, T. N. ed., *Comparative Community Politics*, A Halsted Press.

Clark, T. N., *Urban Policy Analysis: Directians for Future Research*, Saga Publications, 1981.

Clark, W. R. and Hallerberg, M., "Mobile Capital, Domsetic Institutions, and Electorally Induced Monetary and Fiscal Policy", *American Political Science Review*, bol.94, no.2, 2000, pp.323-342.

Chaney, C. K., and Saltzstein, G.H., "Democratic Control and Bureaucratic Responsiveness: The Police and Domestic Violence", *American Journal of Political Science*, vol. 42, no.3, 1998, pp.745-768.

116   References

R. A. Charles, "Recent Conceptsin Large City Administration", in C.B. Edward, *Urban Government: A Reader in Administration and Politics*, revised ed., New York: Free Press, 1969.

Chen, X., "Both glue and lubricant: Transnational ethic social capital as a sournce of Asia-Pacific srbregionalism", *Policy Sciences*, vol.33, 200, pp. 269-287.

Child, J., "Strategies of Control and Organizaitonal Behavior", *Administraitve Science Quarterly*, vol.18, 1973.

Child, J., *Organization: A Guide to Problems and Practice*, Harper and Row, 1984.

Chubb, J. E., "The Political Economy of Federalism", *American Political Science Review*, vol.79, 1985, pp.994-1015.

T. N. Clark, and L. G. Ferguson, *City Money*, Colunbia University Press, 1983.

Cohen, G.A., "Are Freedom and Equality Compatible?" in Elster and Moene eds., *Alternative to Capitalism*, Cambridge University Press, 1989.

Cohen, G.A., "On the Currency of Egalitatian Justice", *Ethics*, vol.99, 1989, pp.906-944.

Coleman, J. J., "Unified Government, Divided Government, and Party Responsiveness", *American Political Science Review*, vol.93, no.4, 1999, pp.821-835.

Costa, D.L. and Kahn, M.E., "Civic Engagement and Community Heterogeneity: An Economist's Perspective", *Perspectives on Politics*, vol.1, 2003, pp.103-111.

Cothran, D. A., "Japanese bureaucrats and Policy Implementation: Lessons for America?", *Policy Studies Review*, vol.6, no.3, 1987, pp.439-457.

Dacon, B. and Hulse M., "The Making of Post-communist Social Policy: The Role of International Agencies", *Journal of Social Policy*, vol.26, no.1, pp. 53-62.

Dagger, R., *Civic Virtues*, Oxford Political Theory, 1997.

Dahl, R. A., *Who Governs: Democracy and Power in an American City*, Yale University Press, 1961.

Daniels, N., "Reflective Equilibrim and Justice as Political", pp.127-154, in Davion, V. and Wolf, C., eds., *The Idea of A Political Liberalism: Essays on Rawls*, Rowman and Littlefield, 2000.

Davies, P.L. and Rose, R., "Are Program Resources to Organizational Change", *European Journal of Political Research*, vol.16, 1988.

Dahl, R., *Modern Political Analysis*, Prentice-Hall, 1963.

Dean H. and Melrose M., "Manageable Discord: Fraud and Resistance in the Social Security System", *Social Policy and Administration*, vol.31, no.2, 1997, pp.103-118.

Dehoog, R. H., Lowery, D. and Lyons, W.E., "Citizen Satisfaciton with Local Governance: A test of Individual, Jurisdictional, and City- Specific Explanations", *Journla of Politics*, vol.52, no.3, 1990, pp.807-837.

References 117

Deller S. C. and Rudnicki E., "Managereial efficiency in local government: Implications on jurisdictional consolidation", *Public Choice*, vol.74, 1992, 221-231.

Demone, H. W. Jr. and Gibelman, M. eds., *Services for Sale: Purchasing Health and Human Services*, Rutgers Univ. Press, 1989.

Derouet, J.L, Dutercq, Y., *L'establissement scolaire, autonomie locale et service public*, Paris: ESF, 1997.

Derthick, M., *Uncontrollable Spending for Social Services Grants*, The Brokings Institution, 1975.

Doyle, M.W, and Sambanis, N., "International Peacebuilding: A Theoretical and Quantitative Analysis", *American Political Science Review*, bol.94, 2000, pp.779-800.

Dreze, J. and A. Sen, *Hunger and Public Action*, Oxford: Clarendon Press, 1989.

Dreze, J. and A. Sen, "Public Action for Social Security: Foundations and Strategy", in Ahmad, E., Dreze, J., Hills, J. and S. Sen, eds., *Social Security in Developing Countries, Oxford Studies in Ancient Philosophy*, Supplementary Volume, 1991, pp. 145-184.

Duncan, G. J. and Hoffman, S. D., "The Use and Effects of Welfare: A Survey of Recent Evidence", *Social Science Review*, vol.62, no.2, 1998, pp.238-257.

Duncan, G. J., Harris, K. M., and Boisjol, J., "Time Limits and Welfare Reform: New Estimatesof the Number and Characteristics of Affected Families", *Social Science Review*, vol.74, no.1, 2000, pp.55-75.

P. Dunleavy, *Urban Political Analysis: The Politics of Collective Consumption*, Macmillan Press, 1980.

Dunleavy, P., *Bureacrats and Democracy*, London: Harvester Wheatsheaf, 1991.

Dunleavy, P., *Politicans, Bureaucrats and Democracy*, London: Harvester Wheatsheaf, 1991.

Dunleavy, P., "Bureaucrats, Budgets and the Growth of the State: Reconstructing an Instrumental Model", *British Journal of Political Science*, vol.15, pp.299-328.

Dunsire, A., *Imprementiation in a Bureaucracy*, St. Martin's Press, 1978.

Dunsire, A., *Control in a Bureaucracy*, St. Martin's Press, 1978.

Dunsire, A., "Central Control over Local Authorities: A Cybernetic Approach", *Public Administration*, vol.59, 1981.

Dunsire, A., "Holistic Governance", *Public Policy and Administration*, vol.5, no.1, 1990.

Dunsire, A., "Organizational Status and Performance: A Conceptual Framework for Testing Public Choice Theories", *Public Administration*, vol.66, 1988, pp.363-388.

During, D., "The Transition from Traditional to Postpositivist Policy Analaysis: A Role for Q-Methodology", *Journal of Policy Analysis and Management*, vol.18, no.3, 1999, pp. 389-410.

118   References

Dye, T. R., *Top Down Policy Making*, Chatham House Publishers, 2001.

Dworkin, R., "What is Equality? Part1: Equality of Welfare", *Philosophy and Public Affairs*, vol.10, 1981, pp.185-246.

Dworkin, R., "What is Equality? Part2: Equality of Resources", *Philosophy and Public Affairs*, vol.10, 1981, pp.283-345.

Dworkin, R., *"Justice in the Distribution of Health Care"*, Clayton M. and Williams A. eds., *The Idea of Equality*, Great Britain: Macmillan Press, 2000.

Dworkn, R., *Sovereign Virtue: The Theory and Practice of Equality*, Cambridge: Harvard University Press, 2000.

Easton, D., *Sytems's Analysis of Political Life*, University of Chicago Press, 1965.

Edwards, B. and Foley, M.W., "Social Capital and Civic Capacity", *Administrative Theory and Praxis*, vol.21, 1999, pp.523-530.

Edwards, G. C. and Sharkansky, I., "Executive and Legislative Budgeting: Decision Routines for Agency Totals and Individual Programs in Two Stats", pp.167-178

Ellis, K., Davis, A., and Rummery, K., "Needs Assessment, Street-level Bureaucracy and the New Community Care", *Social Policy & Administration*, vol.33, no.3, 1999, pp.262-280.

Ettorre, E., "Recognizing Diversity and Group Processes in International, Collaborative, Research Work: A Case Study", *Social Policy and Administration*, vol.34, no.4, 2000, pp.392-349.

Evers, A. and Winterberger, H. eds., *Shifts in the Welfare Mix: Significant Features in Countries with Market Economy*, Westview Press, 1990.

Evers, A. and Svetlik, I. eds., *Balancing Pluralism: New Welfare Mixes in Care for the Elderly*, Avebury, 1993.

Ewald, F., *L'Etat providence*, Paris: B. Grasset, 1986.

Eyestone, R., *Public Policy Formation*, JAI Press Inc., 1884.

Ezra F. Vogel ed., *Modern Japanese Organization and Decision-making*, Univ. of California Press, 1975.

Feick, J., "Comparing Comparative Policy Studies — A Path Towards Integration?", *Journal of Public Policy*, vol.12, no. 3, 1992, pp. 257-285.

Feldman, S., "The Poltical Culture of Ambivalence: Ideological Responses to the Welfare State", *American Journal of Poltical Science*, vol.36, 1992, pp.268-307.

Fitzpatrick, T., *Welfare Theory*, Palgrave, 2001.

Fording, R. C., "The Political Response to Black Insurgency: A Critical Test of Competing Theories of the State", *American Political Science Review*, vol.95, no.1, 2001, pp.115-130.

Forte, F., "The Laffer curve and the theory of fiscal bureaucracy", *Public Choice*, vol.52, 1987, pp.101-124.

Fowley M. W. and Edwards, B., "Is It Time to Disinvest in Social Capital?", *Journal of Public Policy*, vol.19, no.2, 1999, pp.141-173.

References 119

Frederickson, H.G., *New Public Administration*, Alabama Univ. Press, 1982.

Frieden, K., "Public Needs and Private Wants", *Social Policy*, vol.17, no.2, Fall, 1986, pp.19-30.

Fuller, R. and Tulle-Winton, E., "Specialism, Genericism, and Others: Does it Make a Difference? A Study of Speceial Work Services to Elderly People", *British Journal of Social Work*, vol.26, 1996, pp.679-698.

Fukuyama, F., *Trust*, The Free Press, 1995.

Glatzer, W. and Mohr, H.-M., "Quality of Life: Concepts and Measurement", *Social Indicators Research*, vol.19, 1987, pp.15-24.

Gauthier, B., "Client Satisfaction in Program Evaluation", *Social Indicators Research*, vol.19, 1987, pp.229-254.

Gaus, J. M., "Trends in the Theory of Public Administration", *Public Administration Review*, vol.10, 1950.

Gawson, A., *Corporatism and welfare, Social Policy and State Intervention in Britain*, Heinemann Educational Books, Ltd., 1982.

George, P., "Toward a Two-dimensional Analysis of Welfare Ideologies", *Social Policy and Administration*, vol.19, no.1, 1985, pp.33-45.

Gerston, L. N., *Policy Making: Process and Principles*, M.E. Sharpe, 1997.

Charles E. Lindblom and Edward J. Woodhouse, *The Policy-Making Process* (Third Edition), Prentice-Hall, Inc., 1993.

Gibbs, I. and Bradshaw, J., "Dependent and its Relationship to the Assessment of Care Needs of Elderly People", *British Journal of Social Work*, vol.18, 1988, pp.57-592.

Gidron, B., Kramer, R., and Salamon, L. M. eds., *Government and Third Sector: Emerging Relationshipis in Welfare States*, Jossey-Bass, 1992.

Gilbert, N. and Moon, A., "Analyzing Welfare Effort: An Appraisal of Comparative Methods", *Journal of Policy Analysis and Management*, vol.7, no.2, 1988, pp.326-340.

Gilens, M., "Political Ignorance and Collective Policy Preferences", *American Political Science Review*, vol.95, no.2, 2001, pp.379-396.

Gilliatt, S., Fendwick, J. and Alford, D., "Public Services and the Consumer: Empowerment or Control?", *Social Policy and Administration*, vol.43, no.3, 2000, pp.333-349.

Girard, M., Eberwein, W.D. and Webb, K. eds., *Theory and Practice in Foreign Policy-Making: National Perspectives on Academics and Professiionals in International Relations*, PINTER Publishers Ltd., 1994.

Goodnow, F., *Politics and Administration*, Macmillan, 1990.

Gough I., *The Political Economy of the Welfare State*, Macmillan Education Ltd., 1979.

Gough I., "Need Satisfaction and Welfare Outcomes: Theory and Explanations", *Social Policy and Administration*, vol.28, no.1, 1994, pp. 33-56.

References

Granato, J., Inglehart, R., and Leblang, D., "The Effect of Cultural Values on Economic Development: Theory, Hypotheses, and Some Empirical Tests", *American Journal of Political Science*, vol.40, 1996, pp.607-631.

Grand, J. L., *The Strategy of Equality: Redistribution and the social services*, Goerge Allen and Unwin, 1982.

Grand, J.L., C. Popper and R. Robinson, *The Economics of Social Problems*, Macmillan, 1992.

Grand, J.L. and Winter, D., "The Middle Classes and the Welfare State under Conservative and Labour Government", *Journal of Public Policy*, vol.6, no.4, pp.399-430.

Gray J., *Two Faces of Liberalism*, New Press, 2000.

Grossman, P.J., "The optimal size of government", *Public Choice*, vol.53, 1987, pp.131-147.

Gonzalez, R. A. and Mehay, S. L., "Municipal annexation and local monopoly power", *Public Choice*, vol.52, 1987, pp.245-255.

Gough, I. with Thomas, T., "Need Satisfaction and Welfare Outcomes: Theory and Explanations", *Social Policy and Administration*, vol.28, no.1, 1994, pp.33-56.

Greenley, J. R., Jan S. Greenberg, and Roger Brown, "Measuring Quality of Life: A New and Practical Survey Instrument", *Social Work*, vol.42, no.3, 1997, pp.244-254.

Groot, H. D., and Pommer, E., "Budgetgames and the private and social demand for mixed public goods", *Public Choice*, vol.52, 1987, pp.257-272.

Gyford, J. and James, M., *National Parties and Local Politics*, Allen and Unwin.

Gwyn, W. B. and Edwards III, G. C. eds., *Perspectives on Public Policy-Making*, Tulane University, 1975.

Hage J., *Theories of Organizations: Form, Process, and Transformation*, John Wiley and Sons, 1980.

Hage J. and Finsterbusch, K., "Three strategies of organizational change: organizational development, organizational theory and organizational design", *International Review of Administrative Sciences*, vol.55, 1989, pp.29-57.

Hanf, K. and Scharph, F., *Interorganizational Policy Making: Limits to Coordination and Central Control*, Saga Publications.

Hansen, J. B., "Policy-Making in Central-Local Government Relations: Balancing Local Autonomy, Macroeconomic Control, and Sectoral Polic Goals", *Journal of Public Policy*, vol.19, no.3, 1999, pp.327-264.

Hao, L., "How Does a Single Mother Choose Kin and Welfare Support? British Jerry Paul Sheppard, A Resource Dependence Approach to Organizational Failure", *Social Science Research*, vol.24, no.1, 1995, pp.1-27.

Harris, R., "Federal-State Relations in the Implementation of Surface Mining Policy", *Policy Studies Review*, vol.9, no.1, 1989, pp.69-78.

References 121

P. Hay and R. P. Rotunda, *The United State Federal System*, A. Giuffre Editore, Milano, 1982.

Heffron, F., *Organization Theory nad Public Organizations: The Political Connection*, Prentice Hall, 1989.

Heffron, F., "Beyond commuity and society: The externalities of social capital building", *Policy Sciences*, vol.33, 2000, pp.477-494.

Hero, R.E., "Social Capital and Racial Inequality in America", *Perspectives on Politics*, vol.1, 2003, pp.113-122.

Hirst, H., "Democracy and Governance", in Jon Pierre ed. *Debating Governance*, Oxford Univ. Press, 2000.

Hoekstar, V. J., "The Supreme Court and Local Public Opinion", *American Political Science Review*, vol.94. no.1, 2000, pp.89-100.

Holden, M. Jr., "The Competence of Political Science: "Progress in Political Research" Revisited Presidential Address, American Political Science Association, 1999", *American Political Science Review*, vol.94, no.1, 2000, pp.1-19.

Hood, C., *The Limits of Administration*, John Wiley and Sons, 1976.

Hood, C., "*Public Administration: Lost An Empire, Not Yet Found A Role?*", Adrian Leftwich ed., *New Developments in Political Science: An International Review of Achievements and Prospects*, Hants: Edward Elgar, 1990.

Hood, C., "Control Over Bureaucracy: Cultural Theory and Institutional Variety", *Journal of Public Policy*, vol.15, no.3, 1996, pp.207-230.

B., Goodin, R. E., Muffeles, R. and Dirven, H., "*Welfare Over Time: Three Worlds of Welfare Capitalism in Panel Perspective*", *Journal of Public Policy*, vol.17, no.3, 1997, pp.329-359.

Hibbing, J.R. and Theiss-Morse, E., "Process Preference and American Politics: What the People Want Government to Be", *American Political Science Review*, vol.95, no.1, 2001, pp.145-152.

Hill, M., *The Policy Process*, Harvard Wheatsheaf, 1993.

Hill, J. L., and Kriesi, H., "An Extension and Test of Converse's "Black-and White" Model of Respense Stability", *American Political Science Review*, bol.95, no.2, 2001, pp. 397-413.

Hindera, J. J., and Young, C. D, "Representative Bureaucracy: The Theoretical Implications of Statistical Interatiction", *Political Research Quarterly*, vol. 51, no.3, pp. 655-371.

Hogwood, B. and Peters, B.G., *Policy Dynamics*, Wheatsheaf, 1984.

Huckfieldt, R., Sprague, J., and Levine, J., "The Dynamics of Collective Deliberation in the 1996 Election: Campaign Effects on Accessibility, Certainty, and Accurancy", *American Political Science Review*, vol.94, 2000, pp.641-651.

Huemer, M., "Rawls's Problem of Stability", *Social Theory and Practice*, vol.22, no.3, 1996, pp.377-395.

Hughes, B., "A Model for the Comprehensive Assesment of Older People and Their Carers", *British Journal of Social Work*, vol.23, 1993, pp.345-64.

Inkeles, A., "Measuring social capital and its consequences", *Policy Sciences*, vol.33, 2000, pp.245-268.

Ingram, H. and Schneider, A., "Improving Implementation Through Framing Smarter Statues", *Journal of Public Policy*, vol.10, no.1, 1990, pp.67-88.

Jabes J. and Zussman, D., "Organizational culture in public bureaucracies", *International Review of Administrative Sciences*, vol. 55, 1989, pp.95-116.

Jackman, R. W. and Miller, R.S., "The Poverty of Poltical Culture", *American Journal of Political Science*, vol.40, no.3, 1996, pp.697-716.

Jackman, R. W. and Miller, R.S., "A Renaissance of Poltical Culture?", *American Journal of Political Science*, vol.40, no.3, 1996, pp.632-659.

Jankowski, P., *Cette vilaine affaire Stavisky*, Fayard, 2000.

John T. S., Jim, T., and Headrick, B., "Street-Level Political Controls over Federal Bureaucracy", *American Political Science Review*, vol.85, no.3, 1991, pp.829-850.

Johnston, D. F., "Toward A Comprehensive 'Quality-Of-Life' Index, Social Indicators Research", *Social Indicators Research*, vol.20, 1988, pp.473-496.

Johson, N., *The Welfare State in Transition: The Theory and Pracitce of WelfarePluralism*, Harvester Wheatsheaf, 1987.

Judge, K., *Rationing Social Service*, Heineman, 1978.

Jun, J.S., "The Hidden dimension of Japanese Administration: Culture and Its Impact", *Public Administration Review*, vol.55, 1995, pp.125-134.

Kahn, K.F., and Kenney, P. J., "Do Negative Campaigns Mobilize or Suppress Turnout? Clarifying the Relationship between Negativity and Participation", *American Political Science Review*, vol.93, 1999, pp.877-888.

Kagan, R.A., "Understanting Regulatory Enforcenent", *Law and Policy*, vol.11, no.2, 1989.

Kaufman, H., "Emerging Conflict in the Doctrine of Public Administraion", *American Political Science Review*, vol.50, no.4, 1956.

Kaufman, H., *Time, Chance, and Organizations: National Selection in a Perilous Environment*, Chatham House Publishers, 1985.

Keenan, D. nad Rubin, P. H., "The limits of the equal-efficiency tradeoff", *Public Choice*, vol.47, 1985, pp.425-436.

Kenyon, D. A. and Kincaid, J., *Competiton Among States and Local Governments*, Washington, DC: Urban Institute Press, 1991.

Keohane, R. O., "Governance in a Partially Globalized World", *American Political Science Review*, vol.95, 2001, pp.1-13.

References 123

Kjellberg, F., "Local Government Reorganization and the Development of the Welfare State", *Journal of Public Policy*, vol.5, no.2, 1985, pp.215-239.

Lagroye, J. and Wright, V., *Local Government in Britain and France: Problems and Prospects*, Allen and Unwin, 1979.

Laing, J.D. and Slotznick, B., "The pits and the core: Simple collective decision problems with concabe preferecnes", *Public Choice*, vol.66, 1990, pp.229-242.

Lane, R., "Political Culture: residual category or General Theory?", *Comparative Poltical Studies*, vol.25, no.3, 1992, pp.362-387.

Larkey, P.D., Stolp, C. and Iner, M., "Theorizing about the Growth of Government: A Research Assessment", *Journal of Public Policy*, vol.1, no.2, 1981.

Leete, L. and Bania, N., The Impact of Welfare Reform on Local Labor Markets", *Journal of Policy Analysis and Management*, vol.18, no.1, 1999, pp.50-76.

Leibfried, S., "Spins of (Dis)Integration: What Might 'Reformers' in Canada? Learn from the 'Social Dimension' of the European Union?', *Social Policy and Adminstration*, vol.32, no.4, 1998, pp.365-388.

Leigh, D. E., "Can a Voluntary Workfare Program Chage the Behavior of Welfare Recipients? New Evidence from Washington State's Family Independence Program", *Journal of Policy Analysis and Management*, vol.14, no.4, 1995, pp.567-589.

Lipsky M., *Street Level Bureaucracy*, Basic Books, 1980.

Lipsky M., "Bureaucratic Disentitlement in Social Welfare Program", *Social Service Review*, vol. 58, no.1, 1984.

Magnusson, W., "The Local State in Canada: theoretical perspective", *Canadian Public Administration*, vol.28, 1985, pp.575-599.

Mansfield, E.D. Milnere, H. V., and Rosendorff, B.P., "Free to Trade: Democracies, Autocracies, and International Trade", *American Political Science Review*, vol.94, 2000, pp.305-320.

Mansfield, V., *Synchronicity, Science, and Soul-Making*, Open Court Publishing Company, 1995.

Marshall, T. H., *The Right to Welfare*, Heinemann Educational Book, 1981.

Mcbride, M.E., "The economic approach to poltical behavior: Governors, bureaucratis, and cost commission, *Public Choice*, vol.66, 1990, pp. 117-136.

Mcgregor, Jr., E.B., "Politics and the Career Mobility of Bureaucrats", *American Political Science Review*, vol.68, 1974, pp.18-26.

Mcknight, J., *The Careless Society: Community and its Counterfeits*, Basic Books, 1995.

McSwite, O. C., "After Legitimacy: Next Generation Public Administration Theory", *Administrative Theory and Praxis*, vol.21, 1999, pp.409-412.

References

Means, R. and Langan, J., "Charging and Quasi-Markets in Community Care: Implications for Elderly People with Dementia", *Social Policy and Administration*, vol.30, no.3, 1996, pp.244-262.

Meire, K. J., *Politics and the Bureaucracy: Policymaking in the Fourth Branch of Government*, Duxbury Press, 1979.

Meier, K. J. and Mcfarlane, D. R., "Statutory Coherence and Policy Implementation: The Case of Family Planning", *Journal of Public Policy*, vol.15, no.3, 1995, pp.281-298.

Meyre, P., *Administrative Organization: A Comparative Study of the Organization of Public Administration*, Stevens and Sons Limited, 1957.

Meyers, M. K., Glaser, B., and Donald, K.M., "On the Front Lines of Welfare Delivery: Are Worker Implementing Policy Reforms?", *Journal of Policy Analysis and Management*, vol. 17, no.1, 1998, pp.1-22.

Meyers, M. W., "The Two Authority Structures of Bureacratic Organization", *Administrative Science Quarterly*, vol.13, 1968.

Meyers, M. W., *Bureacratic Structure and Authority: Coordination and Control in 254 Government Agencies*, Harper and Row, 1972.

Meyerson M. and Banfield, E.D., *Politics, Planning and Public Interest*, The Free Press, 1955.

Miller, S.M., "New Welfare State Models and Mixes", *Social Policy*, vol.17, no.2, Fall, 1986, pp.10-18.

Mitchell, W. C., "Ambiguity, Contradictions, and Frustrations at the Ballot Box: A Public Choice Perspecive", *Policy Studies Review*, vol.9, no.3, 1990, pp.517-525.

Mishra, R., *The Welfare State in Capitalist Society, Policies of Retrenchment and Maintenance in Europe, North America and Australia*, Harvester Wheatsheaf, 1990.

Moe, T. M., "Control and Feedback in Economic Regulation: The Case of the NLRB", *American Political Science Review*, vol.79, 1985, pp.1094-1116.

Moene, K.O. and Wallerstein, M., "Inequality, Social Insurance, and Redistribution", *American Political Science Review*, vol.95, no.4, 2001, pp.859-874.

Morgan, D. R. and Pelissero, J. P., "Urban Policy: Does Poltical Structure Matter?", *American Political Science Review*, vol.74, 1980, pp.999-1006.

Morgan, G., *Images of Organization*, Saga Publications, 1986.

Montgomery, J. D., "Social capital as a policy resources", *Policy Science*, vol.33, 2000, pp.227-243.

Muramatsu, M. and Aqua, R., *Japan Confronts Its Cities: Central- Local Relations in Changing Political Context*, in Douglas, A. ed., *National Resources and Urban Policy*, Methuen, 1980.

Muramatsu, M. and Naschold, F. eds., *State Administration in Japan and Germany*, Waler de Gruyter, 1996.

References

Muramatsu, M. et al eds., *Local Government Development in Postwar Japan*, Oxford Univerity Press, 2001.

Myles, J., "How to Design a 'Liberal' Welfare State: A Comparison of Canada and the United States", *Social Policy and Administration*, vol.32, no.4, 1998, pp.341-364.

Nagel, S., *The Policy Process*, Nova Science Publishers, Ins. 1999.

Nakamura, R.T. and Smallwood. F., *The Politics of Policy Implementation*, St. Martin's Press, 1980.

Netten A. and Davies, B., "The Social Production of Welfare and Consumption of Social Services", *Jorunal of Public Policy*, vol.10, no.3, pp.331-347.

Nieswiadomy, M. and Slottje, K. H., "An alaysis of the relationship between various redistriutive programs and poverty", *Public Choices*, vol.68, 1991, pp.175-184.

Noam, M.E., "A local regulator's rewards for conformity in policy", *Public Choice*, vol.45, 1985, pp. 291-302.

Noggle, R., "Rawls's Just Savings Principle and the Sense of Justice", *Social Theory and Practice*, vol.,23, no.1, 1997, pp.27-51.

Noble, M., Cheugn, S.Y. and Simth, G., "Origins and Destinations: Social Security Claimant Dynamics", *Journal of Social Policy*, vol.27, no.3, 1998, pp.351-369.

Nussbaum, M., "Nature, Function, and Capability: Aristotle on Political Distribution", *Oxford Studies in Ancient Philosophy*, Suppleentary Volume, 1988, pp.145-184.

Nussbaum, M.C. and A. K. Sen, eds., *The Quality of Life*, Oxford: Clarendon Press, 1993.

Okada, K., *Japanese Management: A Forward Looking Analysis*, Tokyo Productivity Organitzation, 1986.

Oliver, J. E., "City Size and Civic Involvement in Metropolitan America", *American Political Science Review*, vol.94, 2000, pp.361-372.

Olsen, J., *Lessons from Experience*, Scandinavian Univ. Press, 1996.

Osborne, S., *Voluntary Organizations and Innovation in Public Services*, Routledge, 1998.

Ostrom, E., "An agenda for the study of institutions", *Public Choice*, vol.48, 1986, pp.3-25.

Paden, R., "Rawls's Just Savings Principle and the Sense of Justice", *Social Theory and Practice*, vol.23, no.1, 1997, pp.27-51.

Page, E., "Laws as an Instrument of Policy: A Study in Central-Local Government Relations", *Journal of Public Policy*, vol.5, no.2, 1985, pp.241-265.

Papadakis, E. and Bean, C., *"Popular Support for the Welfare State: A Comparison Between Insitutional Regimes,"*, *Journal of Public Policy*, vol.13, no.3, 1993, pp. 227-254.

Parton, N., "Some Thoughts on the Relationship between Theory and Practice in and for Social Work", *British Journal of Social Work*, vol.28, 1998, pp.709-727.

Pateman, C., *Participation and Democratic Theory*, Cambridge Univ. Press, 1970.

Payne, M., *Social Work and Community Care*, Macmillan, 1995.

Peng, I., "A Fresh Look at the Japanese Welfare State", *Social Policy and Administration*, vol.34, no.1, 2000, pp.87-114.

Peterson, P. E. and Rom, M., "American Federalism, Welfare Policy, and Residential Choices", *American Political Science Review*, vol.83, 1989, pp.711-728.

Peters, B.G., "Machinery of Government: Concepts and Issues", Colin Campbell, S. J. and Peters, G. E., eds., *Organizing Governance and Governing Organizations*, Univ. of Pittsburgh Press, 1988.

Peters, B.G., *The Politics of Taxation*, Blackwell, 1991.

Peters, B.G., "Governance and Comparative Politics", in Jon Pierre ed., *Debating Governance*, Oxford Univ. Press, 2000.

Peterson, P.E. and Rom, M., *Welfare Magnet: A New Case for a National Standard*, The Brookings Institution, 1990.

Pierre, J., "Public-Private Partnerships and Urban Governance: Introduction", in Jon Pierre ed., *Partnerships in Urban Governance*, Macmillan Press, .1998.

Pierre, J., Peters B.G., *Governance, Politics and the State*, St. Martin's Press, 2000.

Pigou, A.C., *The Economics of Welfare*, London: Macmillan. 1920, Fourth ed., 1952.

Popkin, S. J., "Welfare: Views form the Bottom", *Social Problems*, vol.37, no.1, 1990, pp.64-79.

Powell, W.W. and Friedkin, R., Organization Change in Nonprofit Organization", in W.W. Powell ed., *The Nonprofit Sector*, Yale Univ. Press, 1987.

Rabin, C. and Zelner, D., "The Role of Assertiveness in Clarifying Roles and Strengtheninig Job Satisfaction of Social Workers in Multidisciplinary Mental Health Settings", *Journal of Social Work*, vol.22, 1992, pp.17-32.

Rabinovitz, F.F., *City Politics and Planning*, Aldine, 1969.

Radcliff, B., "Politics, Markets, and Life Satisfaction: The Political Economy of Human Happiness", *American Political Science Review*, vol.95, no.4, 2001, pp.939-853.

Rank, M.R., "Exiting from Welfare: A Life-Table Analysis", *Social Service Review*, vol.16, no.4, 1987, pp.285-300.

Ranny, A. ed., *Political Science and Public Policy*, Chicago; Markham, 1968.

Ranny, D.C., *Planning and Politics in the Metropolis*, Merrlill, 1969.

Rapoport, R., *Community as a Doctor*, Tavistock, 1960.

References 127

Rawls, J., *A Theory of Justice*, Cambridge, Massachusetts: Harvard University Press, 1971.

Rawls, J., *Political Liberalism*, Columbia Univ. Press, 1993.

Reed, S. R., "Is Japanese Government Really Centralized?", *The Journal of Japanese Studies*, vol.8, no.1, 1982.

Reid, G.J., "Tests of institutional versus non-institutional models of local public expenditure determination", *Public Choice*, vol.70, 1991, pp.315-333.

Rhodes, R. A., *Control and Power in Central-Local Relations*, Gower, 1981.

Rhodes, R. A., *Control and Power in Central-Local Government Relations*, Westmead, Gower, 1982.

Rhodes. R.A., *Understanding Governance*, Open Univ. Press, 1997.

Rhodes. R.A., "Governance and Public Administration", in Jon Pierre ed., *Debating Governance*, Oxford Univ. Press, 2000.

Rich, R. C., "The Representation of the Interest of the Poor in the Policy Process", *Public Policy Across Nations: Social Welfare in Industrial Settings*, JIA Press Inc. 1985.

Richard, S., "Bridging the Divide: Elders and the Assessment Process", *British Journal of Social Work*, vol.30, 2000, pp.37-49.

Robbins, L., *An Essay on the Nature and Significance of Economic Science*, London: Macmillan, 1932; 2nd ed., 1935.

Robinson, E. A. R., Denise E. Bronson, and Betty J. Blythe, "An Analysis of the Implementation of Single Case Evaluation by Practitioners", *Social Science Review*, vol.62, no.2, 1998, pp.285-301.

Robson, W.A., *The Development of Local Government*, 3ed., Alen &Unwin, 1954.

Roemer, J.E., *Analysis Foundations of Marxian Economic Theory*, Cambridge University Press, 1981.

Roemer, J.E., *A General Theory of Exploitation and Class*, Harvard University Press, 1982.

Roemer, J.E., "Equality of Resources Implies Equality of Welfare", *The Quarterly Journal of Economics*, 1986, pp.751-784.

Roemer, J.E., "Egalitiarianism, responsibility, and information", *Economics and Philosophy*, vol.3, 1987, pp.215-244.

Roemer, J.E., *Theories of Distributive Justice*, Cambridge, Mass: Harvard University Press, 1996.

Roemer, J.E., "Equality and Responsibility", Boston Review, WebActive, Electronic Discussion Forum, 1996.

Roemer, J.E., *Commodities and Capabilities*, Amsterdam: North-Holland, 1985.

Rose, R., "The Programme Approach to the Growth of Government", *British Journal of Political Science*, vol.15, no.1, 1984.

Rose, R., *Understanding Big Government*, Saga Publications, 1984.

References

Rose, R., *Ordinary People in Public Policy: A Behavioral Analysis*, London: Saga Publications, 1989.

Rourke, F.W, *Bureaucracy, Politics and Public Policy*, Llittle Brown, 1969.

Wright, V. eds., *Centre-Prefery Relations in Western Europe*, London: George Allen and Unwin, 1985.

Rouke, F.E.ed., *Bureaucratic Power in National Policy Making* (fourth edition), Little, Brown and Company, Boston, 1986.

Sabatier, P.A. and Mazmanian, D., "The Implementation of Public Policy: A Framework of Analysis", *Policy Study Journal*, Vol.8, Special No.2, 1980.

Sacks, S. and W.F. Hellmuth, *Financitg Government in a Metropolitan Area*, Free Press, 1961.

Salamon, L. M., "The Marketization of Welfare: Changing Nonprofit and For-Profit Roles in the American Welfare State", *Social Service Review*, vol.67 no.1, 1993, pp.16-39.

Saslamon, L.M., *Partners in Public Service*, The Johns Hopkins University Press, 1995.

Salibury, R., Urban Politics: The New Convergence of Power, *Journal of Politics*, vol.26, 1964.

Samson C., and South, N., eds, *The Social Construction of Social Policy: Methodologies, Racism, Citizenship and the Environment*, Macmillan Press Ltd., 1996.

Samuels, R., *The Politics of Regional Policy in Japan: Localities Incorporated?*, Princeton Univ. Press.

Samuelson, P. A., *Foundations of Economic Analysis*, Cambridge, Mass: Harvard University Press, 1947, enlarged 2nd ed., 1983.

Sass, T.R., "The Choice of munical government strucure and public expenditures", *Public Choice*, vol. 71, 1991, pp.71-87.

Schandy, N.R., "The Political Economy of Expenditures by the Peruvial Social Fund (FONCODES), 1991-95", *American Political Science Review*, vol.94, 2000, pp.289-304.

Schickler, E., "Institutional Change in the Hourse of Representatives, 1967-1998: A Test of Partisan and Ideological Power Balance Models", *American Political Science Review*, vol.94, no.2, 2000, pp.269-284.

Schlesinger, M. and Lau, R. R., "The Meaning and Measure of Policy Metaphors", *American Political Science Review*, vol.94, no.3, 2000, pp.611-626.

Schmidtz D., and Goodin, R. E., *Social Welfare and Individual Responsibility*, Camgridge University Press, 1998.

Schneider, M., "Intercity competiton and the size of the local public work force", *Public Choice*, vol.63, 1989, pp.253-265.

Schram, S., and Joe, S., "The Real Value of Welfare: Why Poor Families Do Not Migrate", *Politics and Society*, vol.27, no.1, 1999, pp. 39-66.

References 129

Scott, P.G., and Pandey, S. K., "The Influence of Red Tape on Bureaucratic Behavior: An Experimental Simulation", *Journal of Policy Analysis and Management*, vol.19, 2000, pp.615-633.

Seibert, M. T., "Mark A. Fossett, and Dawn M. Baunach, Trends in Male-Female Status Inequality, 1940-1990", *Social Science Research*, vol.24, no.1, 1995, pp.28-62.

Seibert, M. T., Fossett, M.A., and Baunach, D.M., "Trends in Male-Female Status Inequality, 1940-1990", *Social Science Research*, vol.26, 1997, pp.1-24.

Shye, S., "The Systemic Life Quality Model: A Basis For Urban Renewal Evaluation", *Social Indicators Research*, vol.21, 1989, pp.343-378.

Sinclair, I., Stanforth, L., and O'Connor, P., "Factors Predicting Admission of Elderly People to Local Authority Residential Care", *British Journal of Social Work*, vol.18, 1988, pp.251-268.

Selden, S. C., Brudney, J.L., and Kellough, J.E., "Bureaucracy as a Representative Institution: Toward a Reconciliation of Bureaucratic Government and Democratic Theory", *American Journal of Political Science*, vol.42, 1998, pp.717-744.

Sen, A. K. *Collective Choice and Social Welfare*, San Francisco: Holden-Day. Republiched, Amesterdam: North-Holland, 1979.

Sen, A. K., "Rational Fools: A Critique of the Behavioral Foundations of Economic Theory", *Philosophy and Public Affairs*, vol.6, 1977, pp.317-344.

Sen, A. K., "On Weights and Measures: Informational Constraints in Social Welfare Analysis", *Econometrica*, vol.45, 1977, pp.1539-1572.

Sen, A. K., "Utilitarianism and Welfarism", *Journal of Philosophy*, vol.76, 1979, pp.463-489.

Sen, A. K., "Equality of What?", in McMurrin, S., ed., *The Tanner Lecture on Human anner Lecture on Human Values*, vol.1, Salt Lake City: University of Utah Press, 1980, pp.194-220.

Sen, A. K., *Commodities and Capabilities*, Amsterdam: North- Holland, 1985.

Sen, A. K., "Well-being, Agencies and Freedom: The Dewey Lectures 1984", *Journal of Philosophy*, vol.82, 1985, pp. 169-221.

Sen, A. K., *Development as Freedom*, New York: Alfred A. Knoph, 1999.

Sen, A. K., "The Possibility of Social Choice", *American Economic Review*, vol.89, 1999, pp. 349-378.

Sharkansky, I., *Public Administration*, Markham Pub. Co., 1970.

Sheppard, J. P., "A Resource Dependence Approach to Organizational Failure", *Social Science Research*, vol24, 1995, pp.28-62.

Skidmore, M., "Tax and expenture limitations and the fiscal relationshipis between state and local governments", *Public Choice*, vol.99, 1999, pp.77-102.

References

Skocpol, T., Ganz, M. and Munson, Z., "A Nation of Organizers: The Institutional Origins of Civic voluntarism in the United States", *American Political Science Review*, vol.94, no.3, 2000, pp. 527-542.

Smith, K. B., Policy Markets, and Bureacracy: Reexamining School Choice", *The Journal of Politics*, vol. 56, no. 2, 1994. pp. 475-491.

Spriggs,ll, J.F., "Explaning Federal Bureaucratic Compliance with Supreme Cournt Opinions", *Political Research Quarterly*, vol.50, no.3, 1997, pp.567-593.

Steelman, T.A. and Maguire, L.A., "Understanding Particiapnt Perspectives: Q-Methodology in National Forest Management", *Journal of Policy Analysis and Management*, vol.18, no.3, 1999, pp. 361-388.

Suzumura, K., "*Welfare, Rights, and Social Choice Procedure: A Perspective*", *Analysis and Kritik*, vol.18, 1996, pp.20-37.

Suzumura, K., "Consequences, Opportunities, and Procedures", *Social Choice and Welfare*, vol.16, 1999, pp.17-40.

Suzumura, K., "Welfare Economics and the Welfare State", *Review of Population and Social Policy*, vol.8, 1999, pp.119-138.

Suzumura, K., "Welfare Economics Beyond Welfarist-Consequentialsim", *Japanese Economic Review*, vol.51, 2000, pp.1-32.

Suzumura, K. and Y. Xu, "Charaterizations of Consequentialism and Non-Consequentialism", *Journal of Economic Theory*, vol.101, 2001, pp.423-436.

Sosin, M. R., "Administrative Issues in Substitute Care", *British Journal of Social Work*, vol.30, 2000, pp.71-89.

Stoesz, D., "A Theory of Social Welfare", *Social Work*, vol.34, no.2, 1989, pp.101-107.

Stokey, E. and Zeckhauser, R., *A Primer for Policy Analysis*, New York: Norton, 1978.

Swank, D., "Culture, Intitutions, and Economic Growth: Theory, Recent Evidence, and the Role of Communitarian Polities", *American Journal of Political Sicence*, vol.40, no.3, 1996, pp.660-679.

Takao, Y., "Welfare State Retrenchment - The Case of Japan", *Journal of Public Policy*, vol.19, no.3, 1999, pp.265-292.

Tarrow, S., *Between Center and Periphery*, Yale Univ. Press, 1977.

Tarrow, S. et al. ed., *Territorial Politics in Industrial Nations*, Praeger.

Taylor, M., "The Changing Role of the Nonprofit Sector in Britain", in Gidron, B., Kramer, R. M., and Salamon, L.M. eds., *Government and The Third Sector*, Jossey-Bass, 1992.

Therien, J. P. and Noel, A., "Political Parties and Foreign Aid", *American Political Science Review*, vol.94, no.1, 2000, pp.151-162.

Thoening, J.-C., *State Bureaucracies and Local Government in France*, in Hanf, K. and Sharpj, F., ed., *Interorganizational Decision Making*, Saga.

Tindale, C. W., "Rawls's Problem of Stability", *Social Theory and Practice*, vol.22, no.3, 1996, pp.377-395.

References

Tocqueville, A.D., *Democracy in America*, *Paperback*, Vintage, 1961.

Tucker, H. J., "It's About Time: The Use of Time in Cross-Sectional State Policy Research", *American Journal of Political Science*, vol.26, no.1, 1982.

Tufte, E., *Political Control of the Economy*, Princetoy Univ. Press, 1978.

Ungerson, C., "Gender, Cash and Informal Care: European Perspectives and Dilemmas", *Journal of Social Policy*, vol.24, no.2, 1995, pp.31-52.

Viet-Wilson, J., "States of Welfare: A Conceptual Challenge", *Social Policy and Administration*, vol.34, no.1, 2000, pp.1-15.

Vigilante, F. W. and Mailick, M.D., "Needs-Resource Evaluation in the Assessment Process", *Social Work*, vol.33, no.2, 1988, pp.101-104.

Wagshal, U., "Direct Democracy and Public Policymaking", *Journal of Public Policy*, vol.17, no.3, 1997, pp. 223-245.

Waterman, R.W., and Wood, B.D., "Policy Monitoring and Policy Analysis", *Journal of Policy Analysis and Management*, vol.12, 1993, pp.685-699.

Weatherley, R. and Lipsky, M., "Street Level Bureaucrats and Institutional Innovation: Implementing Speceial Education Reform", *Harvard Educational Review*, vol.47, no.2, 1980.

K. C. Wheare, *Federal Government*, Oxford Univ. Press, London, 1951.

Waldo, D., *The Administrative State, A Study of the Political Theory of American Public Administration*, The Ronald Press Co. New York, 1948.

Walsh, K., *Public Services and Market Mechanisms: Competition, Contracting and the New Public management*, Macmillan, 1985.

Waters, M. and Moore, W.J., "The theory of economic regulation and public choice and the determinants of public sector bargaining legislation", *Public Choice*, vol.66, 1990, pp.161-175.

Weisbrod, B., "Toward a Theory of the Voluntary Nonprofit Sector in a Three-Sector Ecnonomy", in Rose-Ackerman, S. ed., *The Economics of Nonprofit Institution: Studies in Structure and Policy*, Oxford Uni. Press, 1986.

Wedeen, L., "conceptualizing Culture: Possibitities for Politcal Sciecne", *American Political Science Review*, vol.96, 2002, pp.713-728.

Whittaker, J. K.," Integrating Formal and Informal Social Care: A Conceptual Framework", *British Journal of Social Work*, vol.16, 1986, pp.39-62.

Wicclair, M. R., "Caring for Frail Elderly Parents: Past Parental Sacrifices and the Obligations of Adult Children", *Social Service Review*, vol.59, no.3, 1985, pp.358-376.

Wildavsky, A., *The Politics of the Budgetary Process*, Boston: Little, Brown, 1964.

Wildavsky, A., "Choosing Preferences by Constructing Institutions: A Cultural Theory of Preferene Formation", *American Political Scinece Review*, vol.81, 1987, pp.3-21.

132　　　　　　　　　　　References

Williams, A. and Anderson, R., *Efficiency in the Social Services*, Basil Blackwell, 1975.

Williams, F., "Race/Ethnicity, Gender, and Class in Welfare States: A Framework for Comparative Analysis", *Social Politics*, vol.2, no.2, 1995, pp.127-159.

Williams, R.," Discretion in Welfare Provision", *Social Policy and Administration*, vol.19, no.3, 1985, pp.242-257.

Willians, O.P., *Metropolitan Political Analysis: a Social access approach*, Free Press, 1971.

Wilson, G., "Co-Production and Self-Care: New Approaches to Managing Community Care Services for Older People", *Social Policy and Administration*, vol.28, no.3, 1994, pp.236-249.

Wood, D.B., "Political-Agent Models of Political Control of Bureaucracy", *American Poltical Science Review*, vol.83, no.3, 1989, pp.965-978.

Wood, D.B. and Waterman, R.W., "The Dynamics of Political-Bureaucratic Adaptation", *American Journal of Political Science*, vol.37. no.2, 1993, pp.497-528.

Wrights, D., *Understanding Intergovernmental Relations*, Duxbury Press, 1978.

Yanow, D., "Tackling the Implementation Problem: Epistemological issues in Implementation Research", *Implementation and the Policy Process*, Greenwood Press, 1990.

Zardkoohi A. and Giroux, G., "Bureaucratic behavior and the choice of labor input: A study of municipal governments", *Public Choice*, vol.64, 1990, pp.185-190.

Zeffane, R. M., "Organization Structures and Contingences in Different Nations: Algeria, Britain, and France", *Social Science Research*, vol.18, no.4, 1989, pp.331-369.

Younis, T. ed., *Implementation in public policy*, Dartmouth Publishing Company, 1990.

****

Bernard, P., *L'Etat et la decentralisation: du prefet au commissaire de la Republique*, Documentation francaise, 1983.

Branciard, M., *Decentralisation dans un pays centralize*, Lyon: Chronique sociale, 1984.

Carlie, U.Y., *Autonomie de la volonte et statut personnel*, Bruxelless: Bruylant, 1992.

Chanson, P., *L'Organization du travail selon Louis Blanc, membre du Government proviso ire en 1848*, l'Institut d'etudes corporatives et socials, 1943.

Deyon, P., *Paris et ses provinces: le defi de la decentralisation, 1770-1992*, Paris, A. Colin, 1992.

References 133

Gruber, A., *La decentralisation et les institutions administratives*, Paris: A. Colin, 1996.

Meny, Y., *Centralisation et decentralisation dans le debat politique francais, 1945-1969*, Libraire generale de droit et de jurispurudence, 1974.

Odion-Barrot, M., *De la centralisastion et de ses effets*, Paris, H. Dumineray, 1861.

Prum, A., *Les garanties a premiere demande: essai sur l'autonomie*, Paris: LITEC, 1994.

Ricoeur, P., *Lectures*, Paris: Seuil, 1991.

Rondin, J., *Le sacre des notables: la France en decentralisation*, Paris: Fayard, 1985.

Rosanvallon, P., *La nouvelle question sociale: repenser l'Etat-providence*, Paris: Seuil, 1995.

Villette, J., *Transprots, decentralisation, 90 pln*, Documentation fancaise, 1986.

Yannakourou, S., *L'etat, l'autonomie collective et le travailleur: etude compare du droit italien et du droit fancais de la representativite syndicale*, Paris: L.G.D.J., 1995.